Grammar of
the Edit

Grammar of the Edit

Third edition

Christopher J. Bowen

Roy Thompson

Focal Press
Taylor & Francis Group

NEW YORK AND LONDON

First published 2013
by Focal Press
70 Blanchard Rd Suite 402
Burlington, MA 01803

Simultaneously published in the UK
by Focal Press
2 Park Square, Milton Park, Abingdon, Oxon OX14 4RN

Focal Press is an imprint of the Taylor & Francis Group, an informa business

Library of Congress Cataloging-in-Publication Data
Thompson, Roy.
Grammar of the edit / Christopher J. Bowen, Roy Thompson.
    pages cm
Revised edition of: Grammar of the edit / Roy Thompson, Christopher J. Bowen. 2009.
Includes index.
ISBN 978-0-240-52600-3 (pbk.) — ISBN 978-0-240-52608-9 1. Motion pictures—Editing. 2. Video tapes—Editing. I. Bowen, Christopher J. II. Title.
TR899.T49 2013
777'.55—dc23   2012037823

ISBN: 978-0-240-52600-3 (pbk)
ISBN: 978-0-240-52608-9 (ebk)

Typeset in Univers
By Cenveo Publisher Services

Contents

Contents

Acknowledgments

I wish to thank the supportive team of publishing professionals at Focal Press who helped make this new and improved third edition a reality. I would particularly like to thank Carlin Reagan who walked me down the home stretch. I hope we continue to honor the legacy of Mr Roy Thompson who penned the first edition so many years ago. The goal we all share in producing this Media Manual is to get the pertinent information about editing motion pictures into the minds and hands of the next generation of visual storytellers. I hope that this revised third edition continues to inform and inspire all those readers who are just beginning their creative journey into the world of motion media production.

As a professor of integrated visual media at Framingham State University, I benefit from being surrounded by fellow educators and a continuously refreshed supply of students in the communication arts. The environment fosters much innovation and new approaches to teaching and learning about our discipline. I wish to acknowledge the support of my colleagues and the helpful contributions from all of my students over the years. The same goes for my experiences when teaching at Boston University and at the Boston University Center for Digital Imaging Arts. A collective thank you to everyone who has added to my growth as an educator and filmmaker.

As a media professional, I wish to thank my many collaborators and clients who have helped me to continue learning and to explore new techniques in telling their unique stories.

I am also grateful to the third edition's proposal and manuscript reviewers for their helpful suggestions and critiques, with a special thank you to John Rosenberg.

Additionally, I would like to thank my on-camera talent for their time and cooperation – Rachael Swain, Caitlin Harper, Crystal Haidsiak, Olivia Lospennato, Jacob Cuomo, Elizabeth Lospennato, Rajiv Roy, Stacie Seidl, Timi Khatra, Wendy Chao, Hannah Kurth, Alexander Scott, Stacy Shreffler, Eliza Smith, Emily Klamm, and Tucker and Ghost. The majority of photographs are by the author with a small but significant contribution donated by Miss Rachael Swain. The line art diagrams and the majority of the hand-drawn illustrations are also by the author. Once again I must offer my thanks and appreciation to Jean Sharpe, who donated her time and skills to illustrating much of the second edition – some of whose illustrations are reproduced here to relive their useful purpose.

Lastly, I acknowledge my family for their support and offer extra special thanks to Emily Klamm who has been there through the thick and thin of it all.

This book is for all people who wish to learn the basics about editing film and video. I hope you have fun and enjoy the ride. If you would like to learn more about the topic, find additional resources, or contact the author, please visit the author's website www. fellswaycreatives.com.

For Emily & Jinx

Introduction

Today's world seems to be filled with screens, both large and small, that stream moving images. From the IMAX™ theatre to the billboard near the highway to your HDTV or laptop or tablet to the smart phone in your pocket – all are capable of displaying motion pictures. And every moving image that you see on these screens has been edited. Movies, television shows, commercials, music videos, web videos of all kinds have been cut down, re-ordered, padded out, massaged, sweetened, and tweaked to some degree or another – by an editor.

A writer creates the story, a director coaches the actors, a cinematographer creates the visual style of each shot, and an editor puts all those pieces together. Being one of the last creative people to touch a motion picture project, the editor truly is the final story-teller. That final version may be exactly what the creators set out to make, or it may be very different in mood, tempo, information content, or emotional effect. It is the skill, craft, and gut instinct of the editor that help form the over-arching visual style, pacing and coherency of story that are ultimately experienced by the audience. Editing is where you get to figure out how to make it all work together.

This text, *Grammar of the Edit*, **third Edition**, continues the series' long tradition of introducing a beginner to the world of motion picture editing. The rules, guidelines, and general practices presented herein will provide a new student of this craft with a solid understanding of the established techniques and methodologies associated with the *What*, *How*, and *Why* of the editing process.

The updated third edition has been thoroughly redesigned and expanded. Most of the figures that illustrate the concepts have been replaced or refreshed. Each chapter begins with an outline of that chapter's contents, and ends with a detailed review section highlighting the main concepts covered by that chapter. New sections called Exercises & Projects and Quiz Yourself conclude each chapter. They present ways you can immediately put into practice the techniques and guidelines discussed in the chapter, and offer a gauge to see how well you absorbed the information. Many new topics have been added throughout and most recurring topics have been rewritten and restructured for clarity and flow.

Some of the major changes or additions are highlighted per chapter:

- Chapter One now contains information on the pacing and manipulation of the visual material, and the topic of Finishing has been added to the phases of post-production section. A general rewrite and reorganization of topics is found throughout.

- Chapter Two receives new photographic illustrations and a general rewrite and reorganization of chapter contents. The Audio Quality topic under the Criteria for Assessment section has been expanded.

- Chapter Three finds expanded topics under the What Factors Lead to Making an Edit section. All subjects have been reorganized with clear headings for best information flow.

- Chapter Four gets a polish and new layout of sections.

- Chapter Five has expanded data on timecode, syncing, and sound editing. It has entirely new sections on Composite Editing, Rendering, Chromakey, Video Resolution, Color Correction, and Importing Still Graphics.

- Chapter Six, the largest and most diverse, presents 49 Working Practices that may be encountered frequently by an editor. Several new topics have been added and a general rewrite, restructuring, and re-illustration has been applied.

- Chapter Seven receives two new discussions on pacing a story and how many elements of that story can be manipulated by the editor. A general rewrite and reorganization of topics is found throughout.

- Appendix A is an all-new listing of internet resources and a helpful bibliography of other filmmaking reference texts from Focal Press.

- Appendix B is an all-new listing of the essential crew positions associated with motion picture production.

- Appendix C is an all-new practice script made available for the reader to record and try out the various editing techniques presented in this book.

Regardless of which direction the fledgling editor will follow, everyone needs to learn how to walk before they can run and this text should help define the basic terms and clarify the common practices of editing. It does not mention specific video editing software but it does discuss some issues inherent to the digital video medium. The term "motion picture" may be used liberally to encompass a variety of project types whether shot for the web, television, or movie theatres. A particular genre of film or a specific type of television programming may be called out in an example to help illustrate a unique point. The goal of this text is to inform a person new to editing about the accepted practices of the craft, the reasoning behind those practices, and how an audience interprets meaning from them. Good technique and not-so-good technique will be discussed and illustrated. In the end, you will find that there is no 100% right and there is no 100% wrong, there is only what works and what does not work – and why.

Chapter One
Editing Basics

- A Very Brief History of Film Editing
- Factors Affecting Editorial Choices
- The Basic Edit Transitions
- Stages of the Editing Process

When you write, you select words from your vocabulary and put them together in a particular way to construct sentences that will inform, entertain, or evoke emotional responses within the reader. When you edit a motion picture, there is a similar process. You have to select shots and string them together in edited scenes to inform, entertain, or evoke emotional responses within the viewer. In order for your written sentences to make sense to readers you must follow the known and accepted rules of grammar for your written language – word order, verb tense, punctuation, phrase and clause construction, etc. There is also a similar visual grammar for the language of motion pictures – it governs how they are shot and how they are edited together.

In our companion book, *Grammar of the Shot*, the basic practices of structure, movement, and purpose in frame composition are discussed in detail. This text, *Grammar of the Edit*, presents the basic guidelines of visual construction that will allow you to take these same shots and assemble them together into a meaningful story. As a creative filmmaker, you may choose to edit your visual elements however you wish, but it should be understood that there are certain basic rules and guidelines that are commonly accepted in the entertainment and visual communication fields. The chapters of this book are designed to help you understand the basic grammar behind the editing process and set you on a path to good editing practices.

A Very Brief History of Film Editing

Long before the existence of digital video and computer editing software, people used emulsion film to create the illusion of movement on a screen. Over one hundred years ago, the newly developed technology of emulsion film strips and hand-cranked moving film cameras were leading-edge technologies, but they only allowed for roughly one minute of any event to be photographed. Many of the original movies were real-time recordings of life's daily events. Very quickly the technologies advanced and the use of motion pictures moved from straight documentary recordings to more elaborately constructed fictional narrative stories. Longer strips of film allowed for longer recording times. As film's visual language began to develop, more shot variety was introduced and motion pictures grew in scope and sophistication. The "cutters" who once just assembled strips of picture film took on a new role. Story structuring – or sometimes reconstructing – became the full-time job of the film editor.

Within just a few decades, a more complex visual language of motion picture photography and editing had evolved. Films were quickly becoming the largest entertainment and information medium on the planet. They were held in high esteem by many and defamed by others as a novelty at best and a corrupting distraction at worst. Motion pictures and how they were perceived by audiences became a source of study. Many theories about the social and artistic values of filmmaking, and the visual power of film editing especially, emerged from different cultures around the world.

At what point the editor cut the film and how the various shots were joined together were seen to have an effect on the viewing audience above and beyond the actual story. Editing was no longer just a means to physically trim the excess footage from a series of shots, but it had become recognized as a powerful tool in the filmmaker's toolbox. The machines that take the pictures and perform the cuts have evolved over time, but most of the basic parameters of visual grammar have remained the same. Differing editorial styles have come and gone, but the core methods and intent behind the practice are unchanged even today.

What Factors may Affect Your Editing Choices?

Editing is the act of assembling individual shots of picture and sound into a coherent story. An **edit**, then, must be the place where you transition from one of those shots to the next shot within that assembly. Put simply, an edit is a cut point – a place where one shot ends and another separate shot begins (see Figure 1.2). The term "cut" stems from the days when motion pictures were shot and edited on very long strips of celluloid plastic emulsion film. Looking at the individual still frames on that strip of film, the editor would determine where to physically cut the film between pictures. A pair of scissors or a razor blade "splicer" was used to actually cut the film at that point (see Figure 1.1). Glue or tape was then used to join the different cut strips of plastic film together again. The cut or join becomes the point of transition from one shot to the next. The straight cut described here is just one way to move between shots. How, when, and why you choose to transition from one shot to another depends on many variables.

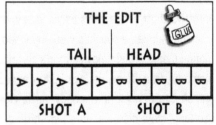

FIGURE 1.1 Initially, editing motion picture film required very basic technologies.

FIGURE 1.2 The head of the film clip for shot B is "edited" onto the tail end of shot A.

The Tools

The first factor you may wish to consider is what medium you are using to perform the physical edits – film, tape-to-tape video, or digital video editing software. Each medium, and the devices that are used in the editing process, can often dictate physical, time-related, or, certainly, financial limitations. At the time of this writing, you would be hard pressed to find anyone who, on a large and consistent scale, still splices emulsion film prints or runs linear tape edit suites. The majority of editing, for all kinds of motion media projects, is done almost exclusively on computers. If you only have access to very basic editing software, then do not worry; you are still able to effectively edit picture and sound elements to create a good story. More advanced tools can allow new editors to play with more bells and whistles, but at the core, you need to maintain good storytelling. Don't believe the hype – the "latest and greatest" technologies do not automatically enhance the quality or value of your project, but you may find it necessary to have a recent version of editing software in order to actually decode and play the video files generated by the many different digital video cameras in use today.

In this book we are purposefully going to keep the discussions of editing grammar as generic as possible. The general rules and practices presented should apply to any medium and to any editing device or application. We will do very little in the way of mentioning specific hardware or software. Just be aware that certain terminology used in one medium may have its origins rooted in another and may vary from one software application to another and even from one country to another.

Project Type and Genre

A second factor that may affect your editing choices can be the kind of project that you are editing. Are you assembling picture and sound media for a documentary, a fictional narrative short film, a news package, a web site's how to video, a music video, a televi sion commercial, a cousin's wedding video, or even an animated cartoon? Each type of motion media project may call for a certain editing style and the use of particular visual elements, transitions, etc. For instance, you may wish to use long, slow dissolves from one shot to the next in a moody music video, but you may not find it very beneficial to use long, slow dissolves in a hard-hitting, factual news package. We will discuss dissolves in more detail later, but the example illustrates the importance of understanding the traditionally accepted guidelines of style for differing program types and for genres within those distinct programs.

The particular type of project you are editing can demand and/or influence the editing choices you get to make. If you are cutting for an established TV show, it probably already has a template or formula to be followed. Watch enough "reality" and non-fiction TV and you'll quickly see the sections, patterns, and timings of each episode. A slow-moving drama may call for uninterrupted long takes of really strong performances by the actors. A promotional video for a motocross racing team may benefit from very fast cutting of short, action-filled clips accompanied by hard driving music and many visual effects (sometimes called **VFX** or **DVE**). Your own experimental film or a music video project could allow you total freedom when it comes to how you treat the visual and auditory elements.

For the purposes of clarity and simplicity, **we will mostly focus on the grammar and practices associated with fictional narrative motion picture storytelling**, but the general guidelines may apply to all forms of motion media.

Degree of Audience Manipulation

It is safe to say that all edited motion media projects are destined to be shown to some kind of audience. The editor is the person who crafts that viewing experience for the audience. It's like taking them on a ride at an amusement park. Are you going to create an adrenaline rush like the corkscrew coaster? Is your project calm like the "kiddie kars?" Do you want to construct a mysterious and involved story full of false leads that is like the hall of mirrors?

The **pacing** and **rhythm** you provide to the shots, scenes, and sequences help control the audience experience and their mental, physical, and emotional reactions to the story. If you present certain information in a certain order for particular durations on screen you will get different responses from the viewer. The need and degree of audience manipulation comes from the **content** and **purpose** of the motion media project. Are you editing an informational Process or How-To video? Not so much direct manipulation of emotions needed. Are you editing a short, funny video for a web site? You might construct a set-up/payoff scenario with comedic timing. A dramatic, action adventure love story has all the ups and downs of a roller coaster ride. Sustained tension needs a release. Suspense must end to feel completed. The script, the direction and the performances (whatever the project might be) all add to the degree of audience manipulation that the editor constructs while assembling the picture and sound elements. Whether the goal of the project is to inform or to entertain, or a combination of both, the quality of the edited content allows the audience to free itself during the viewing experience – to think and to feel – in ways that you, the editor, want them to think and feel.

Other factors involved with editorial choices include your own creativity, the vision of the director, the suggestions of a producer, and the quality of the original visual material that you are tasked with editing together. The right editor can breathe new life into almost any old, tired, or boring material, but an editor, no matter how skilled, may still have to answer to other limiting factors as discussed above. The point is, an editor performs the task of editing but she or he does not always have control over the many variables that are at play during the post-production process.

What Factors may Affect Your Editing Choices?

The Basic Edit Transitions

Let us begin our discussion of editing with the edit point itself.

There are four basic ways one can transition from one shot or visual element into another in your sequence:

- **Cut** – An instantaneous change from one shot to the next. The last full frame of picture for a clip is immediately followed by the first full frame of picture for the next clip.

- **Dissolve** – A gradual change from the ending pictures of one shot into the beginning pictures of the next shot. This is traditionally achieved via a superimposition of both shots with a simultaneous downward and upward ramping of opacity over a particular period of time. As the end of the first shot "dissolves" away, the beginning of the next shot "resolves" onto the screen at the same time.

- **Wipe** – A line, progressing at some angle, or a shape, moves across the screen removing the image of the shot just ending while simultaneously revealing the next shot behind the line or the shape. The wiping shot replaces the previous shot on the screen over a brief duration where both shots are partially visible.

- **Fade** – (1) A gradual change from a solid color-filled screen [typically black] into a fully visible image (aka, fade from black or fade-in). (2) A gradual change from a fully visible image into a solid color-filled screen [typically black] (aka, fade to black or fade-out).

The grammar of the edit has evolved in some ways since the early days of cinema, but these four basic transitions have remained the same. No matter what type of motion media project you are editing or what tool you are using to make it, a cut is still a cut. A dissolve is still a dissolve no matter what pictures you dissolve from and to. A wipe will literally wipe a new shot over the old shot. A fade-in still comes out of black and a fade-out still goes into black. They have remained the same because their individual purposes have remained the same, and almost everyone around the world understands their grammar – or what it means when they see one being used as a transition.

Later in this book you will be able to explore a more in-depth analysis of these basic editing transitions. For now, let us place them aside and focus our attentions on a much broader topic – a general approach to the entire editing process.

Stages of the Editing Process

As an editor, you will be tasked with creating motion media presentations that show coherent, meaningful, emotional, and/or informational "stories" to certain audiences. To achieve repeated successes with these finished sequences, you will, most likely, need to work through several stages of "story" development.

The editing process, more generally referred to as **post-production** (or sometimes just **post**), can range from being rather simple to extremely complex. The post-production period really encompasses any and all work on the project that comes after the shooting (the **production**) is completed. Picture and sound tracks are edited together to show and tell the story, special visual effects are generated, titles/graphics/credits are added, sound effects are created, and music is scored and mixed – all during post-production. On smaller projects, one person may have to do all of this work, but on larger productions, several teams of women and men work in various departments to complete each element and join each phase of the post-production workflow.

In the world of broadcast television editing there are two main phases of post-production – the "**offline**" edit and the "**online**" edit. The offline phase builds out the show completely but it is traditionally done at a lower image resolution so the edit system can work faster. The online phase turns the completed sequence into a high resolution / best audio mix program ready for television broadcasting. It looks and sounds as best as it can for the viewing audience and conforms to the technical specifications of delivery. Today, computer processors, graphics cards, RAM and media drives can be very powerful – that, combined with tapeless video capture and more capable video editing software, lessens the need for rigid offline to online conforming. Most professional and many amateur editors can work on high definition media all the way through the editorial process, although large amounts of drive data storage space are eaten up quickly.

The following is a listing of the major steps involved in a post-production workflow that stresses the editing process for the basic picture and sound elements of a project.

Consider the Acquire to Picture Lock stages as the offline phase, and the Finish and Mastering/Delivery stages as the online phase.

- Acquire
- Organize
- Review and Select
- Assemble
- Cut – Rough
- Cut – Fine
- Picture Lock
- Finish
- Mastering and Delivery

Acquisition—Simply put, you must acquire the visual and audio media recorded by the production team and any other sources required for completing the edited project (i.e., still photos, music, motion graphics, etc.). Motion picture and sound elements, whether on emulsion film, analog tape, digital tape, or as digital media files, must be gathered together for the duration of the post-production editing process. As almost all editing is done on computers, any source material not in a digital form must be converted to a digital format. If you are using a digital non-linear editing system to perform the edit, then you will have to import, capture, or "digitize" all materials as media on your storage drives. These media files must be protected and remain accessible by your editing software for the life of the project.

Organization—All of the minutes, hours, feet, reels, or gigabytes of picture and sound elements should be organized in some way. If you do not have a clear system of labeling, grouping, or sorting all of the material needed for your project, you will eventually have a difficult time finding the appropriate shots or that good sound effect, etc. Having unique bins or folders for material arranged by date, subject, scene and so forth is wise on both short term and long form projects. Organization of source materials is not the most glamorous part of the edit process, but it can certainly make the difference between a smooth post-production workflow and a slower and more frustrating one. Many of the better editors and **assistant editors** are also highly prized for their organizational skills. Tame the chaos into order and craft the order into a motion picture.

Review and Selection—Once you have acquired and organized all of your elements, it will be necessary to review all of this material and pick out the best pieces that will work for your project. You will "pull the selects" and set aside the good stuff while weeding out the junk that you hope you will not have to use. Some editors place the "selects" (or copies of the good stuff) in their "working" bins or folders, while others might color code their clips according to usability. Labeling, in some way, the shots you would like to use will be important as you proceed with the edit. You would also be wise to not actually throw anything away (trash or delete) because you will never know what might come in handy a day or a few weeks into the editing process. That one shot of the flag waving in the breeze may just save the entire edit, so keep it readily available even though you know it is not one of your original selections. Some editors create "Master Footage" sequences out of all the good material so they have a single source through which they may more easily scrub. This is faster than loading each individual clip in the source viewer.

Assembly—This process calls for assembling all of the major pieces of the project into a logical **sequence** of picture and sound elements. If you are editing a scripted story, you may initially try to follow that script as a blueprint for assembling the best selections of the various shots of the scenes that make up the motion picture. Some editors start off by following storyboards or production notes. If you are creating a documentary or even a music video, there is always some story that is trying to be shown to an audience – assemble those raw parts into this skeleton version. No matter what genre the project, the story, in its longest and most rough-hewn form, takes shape now.

Rough Cut—This is a stage of the project's development where the majority of the "visual fat" has been trimmed and you are left with a presentation that is a long but functional version of the narrative, with many rough edges. Not every cut is perfectly timed; there are no finalized titles or graphics; effects, if any, are more or less placeholders; and the audio mix certainly has not been completed. You do have the timing of the main elements down to a good pace, however, and you, and others to whom you show the developing work, like how the story unfolds, although major restructuring of scenes may still occur if the flow does not feel right.

Fine Cut—You have worked and re-worked and massaged the material of your project into a tight and finely tuned presentation. You like the order and timing of shots in each scene, the overall pacing fits the story, and various elements

Stages of the Editing Process

work together as best as they can. There will be no major renovations from this point forward. You, and the majority of the people to whom you show the piece, all agree that only minor tweaks are required. This cut is fine.

Picture Lock—You have reached picture lock when you are absolutely certain that you will not make any more changes to the picture track(s) of your edited sequence. The timing of all picture elements (shots, titles, black pauses, etc.) is set. Once you have locked the picture tracks (sometimes literally but mostly figuratively), you are then free to address your audio mixing needs – final sound effects (SFX), level/panning tweaks, music scoring, etc. In the olden days of actual emulsion film "work print" editing the picture track had to be locked at a precise duration so that each separately constructed audio track would "sync" up from the start frame. All computer editing software is so much more flexible that there is no longer an absolute need for picture lock, but keep in mind that any alteration to overall duration of picture tracks must still be altered on all sync audio tracks as well.

Finishing—Sometimes called the "online edit", Finishing is the stage where the Color Correction (aka, Timing or Grading) of the image is accomplished. Every clip of video is made to look as good as necessary according to the needs of the project (i.e., appropriate colors, saturation and contrast levels, etc.) and exists at the chosen (high?) resolution. The final mixed audio tracks are also in place in your timeline along with these "finished" video tracks.

Mastering and Delivery—All of your efforts in creating a well-edited piece will mean very little if you cannot deliver the show to the audience that needs to see it. These days this process may mean rendering everything and recording your finished sequence onto a master videotape, creating a Cut List for an optical film print for projection in a movie theatre, exporting and converting your story into a computer video file, or authoring onto a DVD or Blu-ray™ Disc. Each medium would require a unique process and supporting hardware, software, and media. The end result is that you have a fully mastered original version of your show that you can then transform into other media formats and upload and/or **distribute** to various viewing outlets for an audience to enjoy.

We should now have a pretty good idea of what the basic editing or post-production workflow is for any project, large or small. You certainly may encounter projects that do not call for all these stages of editing to be executed in a clearly delineated manner, but, for the most part, you will touch upon some combination of each of these stages as you work toward your finished sequence.

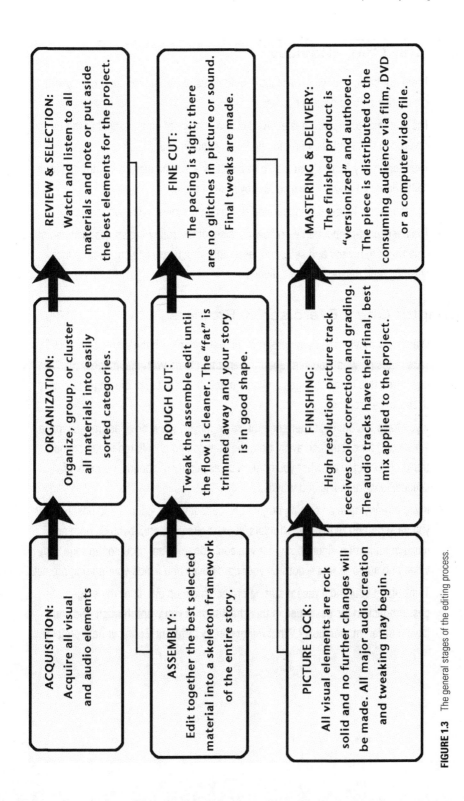

ACQUISITION:
Acquire all visual
and audio elements

ORGANIZATION:
Organize, group, or cluster
all materials into easily
sorted categories.

REVIEW & SELECTION:
Watch and listen to all
materials and note or put aside
the best elements for the project.

ASSEMBLY:
Edit together the best selected
material into a skeleton framework
of the entire story.

ROUGH CUT:
Tweak the assemble edit until
the flow is cleaner. The "fat" is
trimmed away and your story
is in good shape.

FINE CUT:
The pacing is tight; there
are no glitches in picture or sound.
Final tweaks are made.

PICTURE LOCK:
All visual elements are rock
solid and no further changes will
be made. All major audio creation
and tweaking may begin.

FINISHING:
High resolution picture track
receives color correction and grading.
The audio tracks have their final, best
mix applied to the project.

MASTERING & DELIVERY:
The finished product is
"versionized" and authored.
The piece is distributed to the
consuming audience via film, DVD
or a computer video file.

Stages of the Editing Process

FIGURE 1.3   The general stages of the editing process.

Chapter One – Review

1. There are basic and widely accepted guidelines of visual grammar that govern the motion picture editing process.

2. The grammar of the edit has evolved over a century of filmmaking, but the basics, covered in this book, have remained largely unchanged.

3. There are many factors that play a role in how a motion picture is edited, and the editor does not always have control over all of them.

4. The four basic types of transition edits are cut, dissolve, wipe, and fade.

5. The basic post-production workflow consists of the following stages: acquisition, organization, review and selection, assembly, rough cut, fine cut, picture lock, finishing, and mastering and delivery.

Chapter One – Exercises & Projects

1. Watch any movie, television program, or web video with the sound turned OFF. Take notes on what you see regarding anything to do with the images, such as how often the image changes and how many different types of images are used to show the program.

2. If you have the ability, experience the same movie, show or video from Exercise 1 a second time, but face away from the images and only listen to the sound tracks. Take notes on what you hear, such as quality of sounds, quantity of sounds, is there music and when.

3. If you already have an editing project on your computer, open it and observe how you have organized your bins/folders/clips/sequences, etc. If you do not find much organization, figure out what you could do to better group or arrange your video and audio assets – both on your hard drives and inside your editing project.

4. Think about your most recent editing project and map out all of the stages of post-production (as described in this chapter) that you went through. Did you have a different workflow? What might you try differently on your next project?

Chapter One – Quiz Yourself

1. In the early days of filmmaking, how did "cutters" physically attach one strip of plastic movie film to another?

2. What are two factors that can contribute to editorial choices you may have to make?

3. Name the four basic types of Transitions that can occur at an edit point on your picture track.

4. Subjective question: Do you consider a dissolve between two shots or a fade to black / fade from black between two shots to be more dramatic? Why? What factors need to be taken into consideration?

5. List four ways you could organize your video and audio clips in your editing project.

6. If you are in the Assemble Edit stage of post-production, what processes might you be executing at that phase of the edit?

7. During which stage of post-production would you color-correct the video tracks and attend to the final audio mix?

Chapter Two
Understanding the Visual Material

- Basic Shot Types
- Shot Categories – Simple, Complex, and Developing
- Selecting the Best Shots – Criteria to Consider

When you watch a stage play, a music concert, or a sports event in an actual public theatre, club, or stadium, you generally only get to observe the actions of the performers from one static viewpoint – your seat. If any of these events were recorded and broadcast on television, the person watching at home, although missing out on the thrill of being at the live event, will benefit from having a more "intimate" viewing experience thanks to the event's coverage by multiple cameras of varying positions and lens focal lengths. The person at home "sees" more views and details than the person at the actual event.

It is this same concept of coverage that allows people watching a motion picture to feel as though they are observing actual events unfolding before their eyes. They get to "see" more because the camera records the people, places, and actions from many different vantage points that show varying magnifications of detail. Following the Master Scene technique, the production team photographs all of the important action from what they consider to be the most advantageous and necessary points of view. Each one of these camera views is called a shot.

These shots, or individual units of visual information, are eventually given to the editor during post-production. Even though the editor had no control over which shots were recorded on the film set or how they were composed, it will be his or her job to review all of the material and choose the best viewpoints and performances – pull the selects – and combine these various shots to show the audience the best presentation of the story, whatever it may be.

Consider the individual shot types as the vocabulary – the visual phrases – used to edit together complete scenes in a motion picture. Knowing the "words" and their meaning will help an editor construct more meaningful visual sentences.

Basic Shot Types

Most editors get involved with a project only during post-production. Although many professional editors may have worked in production on a film set or in a television studio at some point in their careers, it is not that common for them to work both production and post-production jobs. What is common, however, is the need for editors to know certain production concepts and terminologies and be well versed in the visual grammar of filmmaking. Knowing the basic shot types and how to best juxtapose them during the edit is a key responsibility for the editor. He or she should know how to best "show" the story with these shots. As a review, we present the following section, which highlights and illustrates the main building blocks of cinematic language – the basic shots.

- Extreme close-up (XCU or ECU)
- Big close-up (BCU) [UK] / "Choker" [USA]
- Close-up (CU)
- Medium close-up (MCU) / "Bust"
- Medium shot (MS) / Waist / Mid
- Medium long shot (MLS) or medium wide shot (MWS)
- Long shot (LS) or wide shot (WS)
- Very long shot (VLS) or very wide shot (VWS)
- Extreme long shot (XLS or ELS) or extreme wide shot (EWS)
- Two shot (2S)
- Over the shoulder (OTS) or (OSS)

Shot Descriptions

The basic shot types can be used to record subjects or objects of any size. For demonstrative purposes, we are going to focus our examples mainly on the framing of a human subject. Obviously you will encounter these same shots framing objects or "empty" **film space** without any human figures and you will understand them just the same.

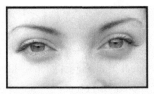

Extreme Close-Up

Big Close-Up / Choker

Close-Up

Medium Close-Up

Medium / Mid Shot

Medium Long Shot

Long / Wide Shot

Very Long / Wide Shot

Extreme Long / Wide Shot

2-Shot

Over-The-Shoulder

Basic Shot Types

FIGURE 2.1 The extended family of film's basic shot types.

Extreme Close-Up (XCU or ECU)

1. Purely a detail shot. The framing favors one aspect of a subject such as his or her eyes, mouth, ear, or hand; may be a magnification of any object or item or merely just a part of an object or item.

2. Lacking any points of reference to the surrounding environment, the audience has no context in which to place this body part or object detail, so understanding will stem from how or when this shot is edited into the motion picture. It is often helpful, but not required, that the subject whose body detail is displayed in the XCU is shown before or after in a wider shot so context may be established for the viewer.

3. This type of extremely magnified imagery can be used in documentary work such as medical films or scientific studies, more fanciful projects like music videos and experimental art films, or it may be used as appropriate in a fictional narrative story.

FIGURE 2.2   Examples of extreme close-up (XCU/ECU) shots.

Big Close-Up (BCU) [UK] / "Choker" [USA]

1. Human face occupies as much of the frame as possible and still shows the key features of eyes, nose, and mouth at once. Top of frame just above eyebrows and bottom of frame just below lips.

2. Such an intimate shot puts the audience directly in the face of the subject. Every detail of the face is highly visible, therefore facial movements or expressions need to be subtle. Very little head movement can be tolerated before the subject moves out of frame.

3. This shot is about who and how that "who" feels – angry, scared, romantic, etc.

FIGURE 2.3   Examples of big close-up (BCU) / "Choker" shots.

Close-Up (CU)

1. Sometimes called a "head shot" because the framing is primarily the face, but it may cut off the top of the subject's hair. The bottom of frame can begin anywhere just below the chin or, more traditionally, with the neck and some upper shoulder visible.

2. A very intimate full face shot of a human subject showing all detail in the eyes. It conveys the subtle emotions that play across the eyes, mouth, and facial muscles of an actor. Health conditions and facial hair in men and make-up use in women are clearly visible.

3. An audience member should be totally focused on the human face. An emotional connection to the on-screen subject can be easily made.

4. This shot shows "who" but not so much where or when.

FIGURE 2.4 Examples of close-up (CU) shots.

Medium Close-Up (MCU) / Bust Shot

1. Sometimes called a "two-button" for the tight bottom frame cutting off at the chest, roughly where you would see the top two buttons on a shirt. Definitely cuts off above the elbow joint. Bottom of frame may be slightly different for men or women, depending on costuming.

2. Character's facial features are rather clear. Where the eyes look is obvious, as is emotion, hair style and color, make-up, etc. This is one of the most common shots in filmmaking because it provides much information about the character while speaking, listening, or performing an action that does not involve much body or head movement.

3. An audience is supposed to be watching the human face at this point in the framing so actions or objects in the surrounding environment should hold little to no importance.

4. Depending upon lighting and costuming, you may discern general information about where and when.

FIGURE 2.5   Examples of medium close-up (MCU) shots.

Basic Shot Types

Medium Shot (MS) / Waist / Mid-shot

1. May also be called the "waist" shot because the frame cuts off the human figure near the waist.

2. Human torso is most prominent in the frame. However, eyes and the direction they look, clothing, and hair color and style are all plainly visible.

3. Subject movement may become a concern because the tighter framing restricts the freedom of gesture. Beware of subject **breaking frame** (an actor's body part touches or moves beyond the established edge of the picture frame).

4. Certainly shows "who" and also provides generic detail about where (inside or outside, apartment, store, forest, etc.) and when (day or night, season).

FIGURE 2.6   Examples of medium shots (MS).

Medium Long Shot (MLS) or Medium Wide Shot (MWS)

1. First shot where the surrounding environment occupies significantly more screen space than the subject. Traditionally framed such that bottom of frame cuts off the leg either just below or, more commonly, just above the knee. The choice for where to frame the leg may depend on costuming or body movement of the individual in the shot. If you cut bottom of frame above the knee, it is sometimes referred to as the "cowboy." (In classical Hollywood Westerns, it was important to get the obligatory "six gun" strapped to the hero's thigh in the shot.)

2. Human figure is prominent and details in clothing, gender, and facial expressions are visible. Environment is clearly conveyed and understandable.

3. Shows who, where, and may still show when.

FIGURE 2.7   Examples of medium long shots (MLS).

Long Shot / Wide Shot (LS/WS)

1. This is usually considered a "full body" shot, wide but still in close to the figure. Often framing feet just above bottom of frame and head just below top of frame. It may often be noted as a generic wide shot (WS) as well.

2. The tall vertical line of the human figure attracts the viewer's eye away from the surrounding environment; however, a fair amount of the character's surroundings is visible and should be considered important to the composition.

3. May work well for an **establishing shot** of a smaller interior location or a contained exterior area like a storefront.

4. Shows where, when, and who. The gender, clothing, movements, and general facial expressions may be seen but real facial detail is somewhat lacking.

FIGURE 2.8 Examples of long shots (LS).

Very Long Shot (VLS) / Very Wide Shot (VWS)

1. Proud member of the wide shot family.
2. May be used in **exterior** or **interior** shooting when enough width and height exist within the studio set or location building.
3. The human figure is visible but only generalities of race, mood, clothing, and hair may be observed. The environment within the film space dominates much of the screen.
4. May be used as an establishing shot.
5. Shows where, when, and a bit of who.

FIGURE 2.9   Examples of very long shots (VLS).

Extreme Long Shot (XLS/ELS) / Extreme Wide Shot (XWS/EWS)

1. Also referred to as an extremely wide shot or a extremely wide angle shot.
2. Traditionally used in exterior shooting.
3. Encompasses a large field of view, therefore forms an image that shows a large amount of the environment within the film space.
4. Often used as an establishing shot at the beginning of a motion picture or at the start of a new sequence within a motion picture. May be cut in whenever a very wide vista needs to be shown in the story.
5. Shows urban, suburban, rural, mountains, desert, ocean, etc.
6. May show day, night, summer, winter, spring, fall, distant past, past, present, future, etc.
7. May show the lone stranger walking into town, or a massive invading army. Most often the human figures in the XLS are so small that details are indistinguishable. General, not specific information will be conveyed about a character.

FIGURE 2.10   Examples of extreme long shots (ELS/XLS).

Two-Shot (2-Shot/2S)

1. Contains two subjects who generally either face toward camera (but not into the lens) or face each other and are seen in profile.

2. Framing depends on whether the subjects are standing or sitting, moving or static, or making gestures and performing actions. A medium 2-shot (M2S) is common but allows for little gesturing or body movement. Medium long shot or long shot two-shots will allow more room around the subjects for movement or action.

3. Framing for tighter shots (MCU, CU) would entail extremely close proximity of subjects' heads, implying intimate connectivity or aggressive posturing like two boxers in a clutch. To see both faces of the subjects in a very tight 2-shot, you would have to "favor" one body before the other, literally overlapping the people within the frame. The person closest to camera and seen fully by the viewer is given favor. No overlapping is required if seen in CU 2-Shot profile, as in a kissing shot, slow dance, or boxers before the match.

4. Adding persons creates a three-shot (3-shot), a group shot, or a crowd shot, depending on how many individuals are clustered together in the frame. The framing would be wider for the extra people who are added to the composition.

FIGURE 2.11   The 2-shot, the overlapping 2S, and the group shot.

Basic Shot Types

Over-the-Shoulder Shot (OTS/OSS)

1. A special 2-shot in which one subject is "favored" by facing camera (either frame left or frame right) and the other subject has his or her back turned toward camera on the opposite side of the frame. The non-favored subject creates an "L" shape at the edge and bottom of frame with the back of her/his head and shoulder; hence the name. The camera shoots over one subject's shoulder to frame up the face of the other subject for the viewer to see.

2. Due to the "shoulder" subject partially cut off at the edge of frame, the shot type used for the OTS may be as tight as a medium close-up – or maybe a full close-up. Anything closer and the composition would alter the balance of the frame and the shoulder may get lost, creating what some may call a **dirty single**.

3. It is often helpful to have a decreased **depth of field** so the portion of the "shoulder" subject visible in the corner of the frame is blurry while the face of the favored subject is well focused. Having a well-focused back-of-the-head may prove to be distracting for the audience. Editing software Matte and Blur effects can help with this if needed.

FIGURE 2.12 Examples of over-the-shoulder (OTS) framing.

Shot Categories – Increasing Complexity of Images

It is worth noting that all of the shot types outlined above have one thing in common: they belong to an over-arching shot category that we will call "**simple** shots." They could, however, evolve into two other categories – **complex** shots or **developing** shots. Before we clarify what constitutes a simple, complex, or developing shot, we should give just a bit of attention to the four basic elements of shot creation whose presence helps determine into which category a shot may be placed.

> LENS—Does the camera's lens move during the shot? Does the lens alter its light-gathering characteristics while the shot is being recorded? Because the camera is stationary, lens movement can only be achieved when using a **zoom** lens. So you have to determine if there is a zoom or a **focal length** change during the shot (Figure 2.13).

> CAMERA—Does the entire camera body move during the shot? Essentially, is there a panning action or a tilting action executed while the camera is recording the shot? The camera mount (**tripod head**) would have to allow for these horizontal and vertical axis changes, but the camera support (**tripod**) would not be in motion (Figure 2.14).

> MOUNT/SUPPORT—Does the camera's mount or support physically move the camera around the film set or location during a shot? In a television studio the camera is mounted atop a **pedestal,** which can boom up (raise camera height) or boom down (lower camera height) and roll around the smooth floor. On a film set, the camera can be mounted to a moving **dolly** or a **slider** on tracks (for **crab** or **truck** moves), it can be attached to a **crane** or **jib arm**, or suspended from cables, or carried with a Steadicam, and so forth (Figure 2.15).

> SUBJECT—Does the subject being recorded move during the shot? The subject can be a person or many people, an animal, an animated object (something non-living capable of movement, like a remote-controlled toy car), or an inanimate object (something that does not move, like a brick or a pirate's treasure chest) (Figure 2.16).

Because you, as the editor, were not on set during production you will not definitively know which shots contain these four elements. Most often their presence or lack thereof will be noticeable to some degree because they all involve movement of some kind. What you should understand, though, are the basic categories that shots will fall into when one or several of the four elements are present. These three basic categories are **simple shots**, **complex shots**, and **developing shots**. Defining these over-arching

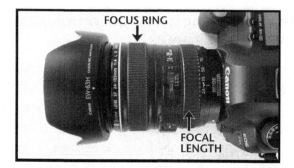

FIGURE 2.13 A camera lens with zoom or vari-focal capabilities.

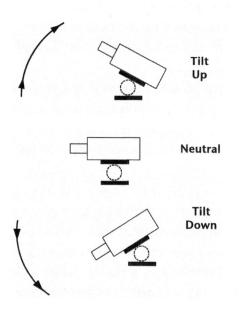

FIGURE 2.14 Camera mounted to pan/tilt tripod head.

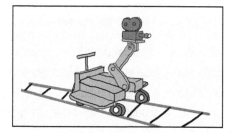

FIGURE 2.15 A camera on a dolly.

FIGURE 2.16   Subjects in motion and at rest.

shot categories now will help us in our analysis of editing them together – a topic we cover later in this book.

Simple Shots

- No lens movement
- No camera movement
- No mount movement
- Simple subject movement

Simple shots are just that – simple. They have no focal length changes (zooms). They have no tilting or panning actions. They show no camera body movement, as with a dolly or a jib. They do show the subject move in simple ways across screen, standing, sitting, speaking, etc. The basic shot types, discussed earlier, are all covered from a particular angle, with a set focal length on the lens and a **locked-off** mount. Whatever simple action unfolds before the camera, it happens within that set and finite framing. Often, simple shots can make up the bulk of fictional narrative motion picture content that is dialogue driven (Figure 2.17).

Shot Categories – Increasing Complexity of Images

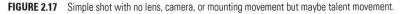

FIGURE 2.17   Simple shot with no lens, camera, or mounting movement but maybe talent movement.

Complex Shots

- Lens movement
- Camera movement
- No mount movement
- Simple subject movement

A complex shot may contain a:

- Pan
- Tilt
- Pan and tilt (diagonal upward or downward camera lens movement)
- Lens movement (zoom or a focus pull)
- Lens movement and a pan (hiding a zoom by panning the camera)
- Lens movement and a tilt (hiding the zoom by tilting the camera)
- Subject movement and a pan
- Subject movement and a tilt

If a shot contains any combination of the three active elements (lens movement, camera movement, or simple subject movement), then it may be considered a complex shot.

If the complex shot does contain a **pan** or a **tilt** then the production team should have ensured that it begins with a static start frame, goes through its move, and completes with a static end frame. The static start and end frames of these pan and tilt shots are very important to the editor. You will find that it may be difficult to cut from a static shot into a shot already in motion, or cut out of a motion shot to a static shot. Entering or leaving movement at the cut can be very jarring for an audience. The best-case scenario is for you to be presented with pan and tilt shots that start and end with static frames and contain smooth even movement in between.

Developing Shots

- Lens movement
- Camera movement
- Mounting movement
- More complex subject movement

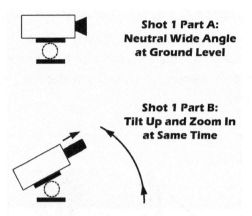

Shot 1 Part A:
Neutral Wide Angle
at Ground Level

Shot 1 Part B:
Tilt Up and Zoom In
at Same Time

FIGURE 2.18   A complex shot can combine a zoom with a camera tilt and subject movement.

A developing shot incorporates movement on all four elements. As such, you can imagine that these shots are rather difficult to accomplish. Subjects may move in complicated blocking patterns on set, the camera is moved about on a mount (perhaps a dolly, a Steadicam, or a crane boom arm, etc.), the lens is being re-focused or perhaps zoomed, and there will be a panning or tilting action at some point to follow the action.

As an editor, you should watch these developing shots very carefully for quality assurance. They will most likely start and end with static frames, but the middle portion could be a hodgepodge of actions. Watch for proper focus, good framing, and smooth movements. These types of elaborate developing shots are designed by the filmmakers to be used as one stunning show piece, so there is often little actual editing that you may need to do beyond cutting the shot into the overall scene at the appropriate point. Cutting into and out of moving developing shots can upset the flow of the entire shot and take away from its effect on the viewing audience. This may be necessary for creative purposes, or if some of the action within the developing shot is not top quality – or if there is a lot of good coverage available to show a very dynamic action sequence.

A specific example of a developing shot is known by many names but perhaps most famously as the "Vertigo" shot. Alfred Hitchcock incorporated this type of in-camera visual effects shot in the 1958 Paramount Pictures release *Vertigo*. The camera either dollies toward a subject while simultaneously zooming wider or dollies away from the subject while zooming in. The goal is to keep the "foreground" object (the subject) the

Shot Categories – Increasing Complexity of Images

same size in the frame throughout the move. The result is a "warping" of perspective/ magnification on the visible background elements in the shot. The audience is made to feel uneasy because of this unnatural visual trick. It is often used in filmmaking to indicate a disquieting, imbalanced or freaky feeling for that character or within the narrative at that moment.

FIGURE 2.19   A developing shot follows complex action with lens, camera, and mounting movement.

Selecting the Best Shots

We should all feel comfortable now identifying the various types of shots that may be used to record the images of a motion picture. With these committed to memory, it will be that much easier to organize them when you acquire and review the visual media to be edited. Be forewarned, however, that not every shot type may be used to generate coverage for a particular scene. For example, it may not make much sense to look for an XLS in footage from a dialogue scene shot in an airplane cockpit.

Once you have the material organized, it will be helpful to review each shot for its technical and aesthetic qualities. Certain criteria work for some motion picture genres, but not all movies, shows, commercials, or music videos can be held up to one master checklist of good or bad qualities. What might never be allowed as acceptable in one program type may be entirely encouraged in another. So, as an editor, you will have to make your own judgment calls depending on the type of project you are editing and what the end goals of that project are set to be.

What Could Make or Break a Shot? Criteria for Assessment

Beyond judging whether your shots fall into the categories of simple, complex, and developing, you should be watching them for a level of quality assessment. The listing that follows, although certainly not exhaustive, should provide plenty of criteria upon which you might base an analysis of the material you will be editing. Again, the type of video you have to edit will often come with its own style, traditions, and sense of what is acceptable and what is not, but you should at least be aware of these potential "gotchas."

- Focus
- Audio quality
- Exposure and color temperature
- Framing and composition
- Screen direction
- 180 degree rule

- 30 degree rule
- Matching angles
- Matching eye-line
- Continuity of action
- Continuity of dialogue
- Performance

Selecting the Best Shots

Focus

One of the chief issues that you may encounter as an editor is incorrect focus during a shot. Nothing can ruin a good performance like bad focus. It is the camera department's job to ensure good focus on shots, and, for the most part, they will. It only takes one false move or late start with the focus pull to turn a potentially good take into a bad one. With scripted fictional narrative filmmaking, the production team will often shoot multiple takes of a line reading or an action to ensure that they have the focus correct, so you should not have to worry too much with that kind of material. Unscripted projects, such as documentaries, corporate interview videos, or live news, often only have one chance at good focus while the action happens in front of the camera. A soft-focus talking head interview could render that entire interview unusable.

Why is soft focus or blurry imagery so bad? It is the one technical factor in film or video that cannot be corrected during post-production. Unlike exposure, color correctness, or even framing, there is no fix for soft-focus footage. It becomes a problem because the viewing audience is intolerant of blurry images. As humans, our visual system is set to always see things in sharp focus (unless, of course, you require glasses or other corrective lenses to properly focus the light in your eyes). When we watch a moving image that has soft focus, we become distracted and uncomfortable as our eyes try to focus on the image that cannot resolve. It is unnatural for us to see things as being blurry. When a filmmaker purposefully causes things to go blurry in a shot, it should have a thematic meaning. There usually is a subjective motivation for the blur (a drugged or injured character POV for instance). If this does happen, placing some object within the frame in good focus should quickly follow it or the editor should cut to a different in-focus shot within a reasonable time. So, unless you are experimenting with radical focus shifts while shooting footage for a music video, you should avoid using blurry takes when you edit.

FIGURE 2.20 Audiences may forgive many things about an image, but they do not tolerate blurry pictures. Use the shots that have the best focus.

Audio Quality

Any sound sources, whether from videotape, a digital recorder, or digital media files, must be of good quality in order to use them in the final **audio mix**. This holds especially true for any of the synchronous dialogue recordings from the production footage.

Some obvious issues to listen for:

- Levels – Adequate volume; not too quiet and not too loud (over-modulated) (Figure 2.21).
- Presence – Does the audio recording match the image size? If it is a CU, do the words sound like they are up close also? If it is a long shot, does the audio represent the correct distance perspective?
- Hiss – Is there any background (electronic) "hiss" or buzzing, etc., in the audio signal?
- Overlap – Do the actors speak over each other's lines of dialogue? You cannot isolate an individual's line delivery if many subjects are speaking all at once.
- Ambience Pollution – Unwanted sounds from the recording environment such as jet engines, air conditioner motors, traffic, radios or music, footsteps, conversations, etc.
- Does it exist? – Some technical issues (batteries, cabling, switches not switched, etc.) can result in no audio being recorded while the picture is recorded. You may find that the corresponding audio for a picture track you have was simply never recorded.

Unlike bad focus, there are some tricks that can be done to improve the sound quality of the audio. Video and audio editing software applications usually have simple controls for managing the easy stuff like levels and panning. Special audio filters or effects also exist to handle the more challenging audio signal manipulations (e.g., pitch shifting, time compression, reverb, etc.). If the audio is really bad and cannot be salvaged by tweaking with the audio software, then you still have the option of replacing it entirely with new, cleanly recorded dialogue audio files that will match the picture exactly. Some refer to this as **looping** or **automated dialogue replacement** (**ADR**). An audio engineer is more likely to do this re-recording work with the acting talent, but the editor would most likely edit the ADR audio tracks into the timeline. Of course, on small projects you would have to do all of this yourself. So if the pictures are good, but the audio is bad, the media may still be usable — depending on the project, time, and availability of talent — for post dubbing.

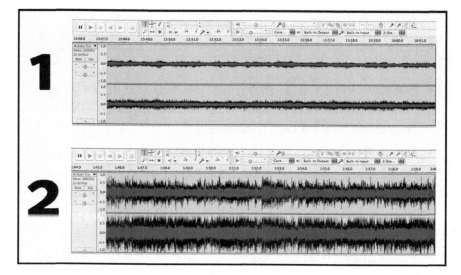

FIGURE 2.21 Choose material with the best audio first. Example 1 shows an audio clip that was recorded with very low levels. Example 2 shows an audio clip with very high levels. There may be ways to do a simple fix with audio "sweetening" software.

Exposure and Color Temperature

With the availability of powerful yet relatively inexpensive video editing software, issues with the **exposure** and **color temperature** of the images are no longer that difficult to fix. Of course, you would prefer that all shots were originally recorded with good exposure and had the proper "look" for the color palette of the project's visual design. If these shots exist in the master footage, then you really should start by selecting those first. But, if good performances or other visual material is present on shots that have exposure issues (overall image is too bright or too dark) or color temperature shifts (image looking overly blue or overly orange, etc.), then keep those shots for use and have yourself or a video colorist attend to their corrections with the software tools available. Even the most rudimentary video editing software has some controls for altering image quality for **luminance** (brightness and contrast) and **chrominance** (hue and saturation).

Audiences do not like it if someone has green skin when there is no reason in the story for that character to have green skin. Additionally, consider your own editing needs. How would it look to cut back and forth from a dark shot to a very bright shot if these separately recorded images are a part of the same scene, the same physical film space. Our eyes and our brains could be missing valuable information as we try to adjust between and rationalize the extremes of dark and light. For everyone's sake, either correct the exposure and color issues or do not use the footage in the final project, if at all possible.

FIGURE 2.22   Select the well-exposed shots. If you have to edit using dark or light shots, most video editing software comes with some built-in exposure and color correcting tools to help.

Framing and Composition

Living at the cusp between a technical issue and an aesthetic issue is the framing of a shot. It can be considered technical in the sense that sometimes the format of the recording device (film or video camera) may be a different size than the frame of the final deliverable product. This is especially true today if a project will contain miniDV/16 mm film elements, which have a traditional aspect ratio of **4:3** for **standard definition** (**SD**). Finishing the mixed aspect ratio video for widescreen **16:9 high definition** (**HD**) may call for some framing adjustments in post. As an editor, you may be called upon to **reformat** the video frame (scale it, "letterbox" it, cut it down to a smaller size as a PIP or split screen element, etc.). Less likely these days, you may have to perform what is called a **pan and scan**, where you take a wide screen camera original format and extract a smaller frame size from it while simultaneously panning left and right to maintain some semblance of good composition in the new, smaller image. If you are mixing SD material into an HD project you may choose to "pillar box" the 4:3 picture inside the 16:9 frame size. (see Figure 2.23)

Aesthetic criteria for framing and composition have fewer immediate fixes. You will have to watch complex and developing shots for good focus, but also for good framing and proper composition. If an elaborate camera move bumps, jumps, sways, or in some way misses its mark while covering talent or action, then you should not consider using that particular take, or at least not that particular portion of that take. Again, during production, there are normally quality controls for reviewing each shot, and if the filmmakers do not get it right they usually perform the shot again, so you should have at least one good choice for your edit, but not always. That is where creative cutting comes into play.

Of course, you will also wish to gauge the qualitative attributes of a shot. Is there appropriate **head room**? Is there appropriate **look room** or **looking room**? Is the **horizon line** parallel to the top and bottom edges of the frame (if it should be)? Do you think the eye-line works? Is the vertical **camera angle** too high or too low? Is the horizontal camera angle too **subjective** or too **objective**? Does it work with the type of project you are editing? Very few of these other aesthetic qualities of the shots can be fixed by the editor (short of using some software effects to resize or rotate an image) so it might be best to place them on the back burner and use any other better takes if you have them.

Screen Direction

This is mostly an issue with scripted fictional narrative media, but it comes up in other genres as well. Talent or subject movement out of the frame of one shot and into the frame of another shot must maintain consistent screen direction. To clarify, frame left is screen left and frame right is screen right when watching the images. The film space itself, the world in which the characters live and move, must be considered as real space; therefore it must comply to the same rules of left, right, up, down, near, far, etc.

If shot A shows a character exiting frame left, then, when you cut to shot B, the same character should be entering from frame right. The character's direction of movement within the film space should be consistent – right to left and right to left again (see Figure 2.24). If you show a character exiting frame left in shot A, then show the same

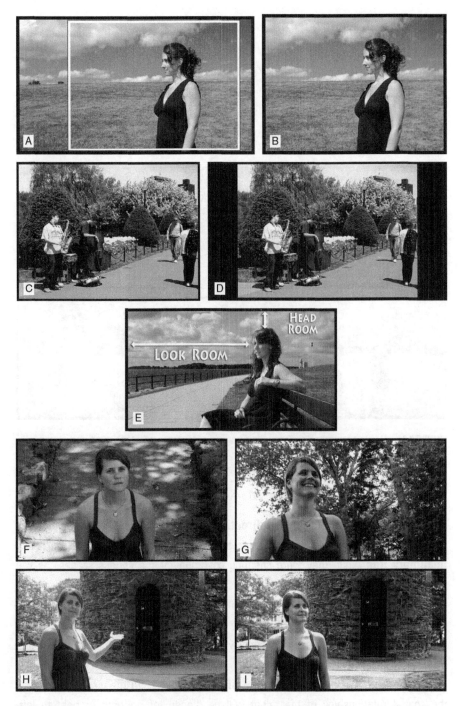

FIGURE 2.23   (A–B) An example of an SDTV 4:3 extraction from an HDTV 16:9 widescreen image. (C-D) An example of a 4:3 "Pillar Box" inside a 16:9 frame. (E) An example of a frame with good head room, look room, and a visible horizon line. (F–G) High and low angles on a subject. (H–I) An example of subjective camera style and objective shooting coverage.

character *entering* from frame left in shot B, it will appear as though the character has simply turned around and is magically re-entering a different location. Some schools of thought say "anything goes" in today's motion media world of movies, television, and web videos. They are counting on the viewing public's sophistication in understanding cinematic language. This may be, but you can never go wrong with maintaining proper screen direction – allowing for deviations if the genre calls for it.

FIGURE 2.24   Maintaining screen direction of talent movement between shots helps orient the viewer within the film space.

180 Degree Rule/Axis of Action

Continuing the logic of our **screen direction** discussion, you must also analyze the footage to make sure that the production team respected the **axis of action** or the **imaginary line** while they were shooting coverage for the various scenes. As you may know, the 180 degree rule is established from the first camera set-up covering the action of a scene, which is usually a wide shot showing the subjects and their environment. An imaginary line, following the direction of the talent's **sight line**, cuts across the set or location and it defines what is frame left and what is frame right. Each successive medium or close-up shot of the talent within the scene should all be set up on the same side of this **line of action** or else, to the viewing audience, the spatial relationships of the talent will be flipped left to right or right to left. Traditionally, screen direction is maintained by shooting all the coverage from the one, initial, side of this line.

If you consider one of the alternate names for this practice, the **180 degree rule**, it might help clarify what is going on. When the camera crew records a two-person dialogue scene for the wide shot, they have established the side of the set or location from which they will continue to shoot all of the remaining shots needed for coverage. The imaginary line, set up by talent sight lines, bisects an imaginary circle around the talent and makes a semi-circle within which the camera can move for more shooting. Should the camera move across the line to shoot an individual's close-up, that character, once edited into the scene, will appear to be turning and facing the opposite direction. This will look incorrect to the audience because this shot will break from the established screen directions for this scene. As a result, you really should be careful if you are looking to edit in a shot that has **crossed the line**.

Many filmmakers today are rather relaxed with this "rule." A free-form approach to talent and camera movement, plus the sophistication of the viewing audience, allow for some switches within the scene coverage. Although you may never go wrong in using the traditional action line guide, use the shots that fit the editing style of the scene and go for the strongest performances.

30 Degree Rule

Based around the concept of the 180 degree rule, the **30 degree rule** calls for the camera crew to move the camera around the 180 degree arc by at least 30 degrees before they set up for a new coverage shot of talent. The reason is simple. If two shots, say a medium long shot and a medium shot, of one person are shot from two locations around the 180 degree arc and the physical distance between camera set-ups is less than 30 degrees, then the two shots, when cut together by the editor, will look too similar on the screen and cause a "jump" in the mind of the viewer.

This is one example of how a **jump cut** can occur. Without sufficient movement around the shooting arc, the viewpoint that the camera offers is too similar to the previous one and the subject will occupy nearly the same frame space. If you have to edit these two similar shots together, the imagery will appear to suffer an immediate jump in space and possibly in time. The angles of coverage and the shot type must be different enough to allow a believable alteration in view points across the cut. As the editor, you cannot control where the camera was placed for the close-up coverage, but you do have control over what two shots you juxtapose together at a cut point, provided there are more than two angles of coverage. Make sure that the two shots are sufficiently different enough in **angle on action** so they do not appear to "jump" while viewing them across the edit.

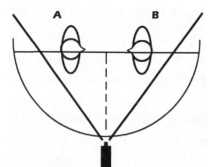

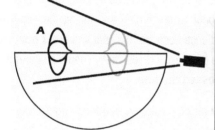

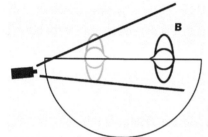

Crossed over the Action Line

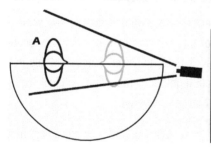

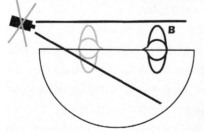

FIGURE 2.25 Coverage shots that "cross the line" may not be usable because they break the established screen direction for the scene. The two characters end up looking across the screen in the same direction rather than back and forth at one another.

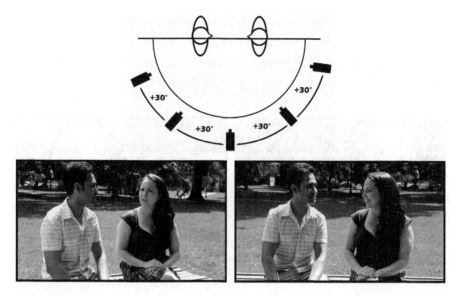

FIGURE 2.26   It is best to edit coverage shots whose individual angles on action are greater than 30 degrees apart along the 180 degree arc. If the camera angles covering the action are too similar, as in this example, the audience will perceive the edit as a type of jump cut.

Matching Angles

When shooting dialogue scenes, the production team will most often shoot what are called **matching angles** – coverage of each character in each shot type where the angle on the person, her/his size in the frame, the lighting scheme, and the focus on the faces are all consistent with one another. One person's close-up will look very similar to the other person's close-up, but they will be on opposite sides of the frame.

Traditional Master Scene filmmaking technique has historically called for an "outside – in" construction of a scene's progression from beginning to end. Although not adhered to as much these days, it is a tried-and-true technique that will work for almost any motion picture. As an editor, you might assemble a traditional scene something like this:

- Establishing shot – A very wide shot showing the location where the scene is to take place
- Wide shot – Showing the characters involved in the scene
- Closer 2-Shot – Bringing the two characters together in a tighter framing
- Over-the-Shoulder of first character
- Answering OTS of the other character
- Medium Close-up of first character
- Answering Medium Close-up of second character

Cutting back and forth between matching coverage shots (OTS, MS, CU, etc.) will be easily accepted by the viewing audience because the images, although of two different people on opposite sides of the screen, "answer" one another and look like they belong together – responding to one another. In other words, they match.

FIGURE 2.27   Use matching angles of shot types when editing coverage for a scene involving more than one person.

Matching Eye-line

Eye-line (**sight line**) is an imaginary line that connects a subject's eyes to whatever object holds his or her attention within the film world. If two people are speaking with one another, the other person's face or eyes are often the object of interest, so the eye-line would **trace** from character A's eyes to character B's face/eyes. It could be a person looking at a clock, or a dog, or a work of art, etc. Getting the audience to trace the eye-line from a character in a close framing to an object of interest not in the same frame can be tricky. When you cut away from the shot of the person looking to the shot of the object of interest, the eye-line must match (see Figure 2.28). An audience member must be able to trace the imaginary line from the subject's eyes to the object across the cut point and into the new shot. If this line does not flow correctly, then the audience will feel like something is just not right. As an editor, you cannot really fix eye-line mistakes; you will just have to find some other way to cut around the issue (see the use of **inserts** and **cut-away** shots later in the text).

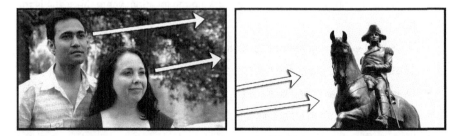

FIGURE 2.28   The eye-line or imaginary lines of attention should match across the cut point between two shots.

Continuity of Action

We will discuss this in greater detail later in the book, but it is a topic that frustrates many editors. The action performed by or around the talent in one shot should match, relatively exactly, the same action performed in a different angle within the same scene's coverage. This is called an Action Edit. Humans are very good about determining fluidity of motion. When things do not flow – when supposedly continuous actions do not match across a cut point – it is easily noticed (see Figure 2.29). Your job will be to finesse these action cuts as best as possible. Unless there is an obvious glitch in one entire shot, you may not be able to tell that actions will not match until after the footage review stage. Save all the good takes and see which ones eventually cut best with one another. Trimming just a frame or two from the tail of one shot or from the head of the next might be able to smooth over minor errors in continuity of action, but anything major will need to be addressed by other, more creative editing options – perhaps a simple cut-away or a customized effect – that fit the style of the project.

FIGURE 2.29 Be watchful of continuity issues within the shots you are considering for the edit. Here, the water bottle jumps hands across the cut point.

Continuity of Dialogue

Be aware of actor line delivery when reviewing the footage. Does the talent say different words from take to take and shot to shot? Is there a different timbre in the voice or a modified rate of delivery? Directors will often encourage actors to try different emotions, tactics, and approaches to what and how the character is speaking and behaving. These variations can be a goldmine if they all work together in the scene. If they cannot be joined together, then the editor will be faced with some challenges. Laying in different audio from alternate takes may alleviate some of these issues, but sometimes things just will not match. As with most audio issues, there may be a way around them for a fix, so keep the footage for later use. Ultimately, you and the director may decide that going with the best performance is better than sticking with action or dialogue continuity within a scene.

FIGURE 2.30   Lines of dialogue that stray from the script may come from inspired performances and even create a better story.

Performance

The performance an actor delivers on the film set is certainly an issue that the editor has absolutely no control over – that is decided between the actor and the director. You cannot fix bad acting or bad direction of good actors. You can, however, hide it or mask it through creative editing. As the editor, you set the pacing of the scene, the order and timing of line delivery, and, through the juxtaposition of clips of varying performances, you can alter the tone, mood, or perceived behavior of a character. You decide which performance works best in the edited story. Sometimes there simply is nothing else to cut to and there are no "better" takes to use. Cut in what you think works best for the overall scene, grin and bear it, and move on. If the talent performance is actually very strong but their ability to match their **business** (holding a glass or cigar, brushing their hair, etc.) is what makes a certain take less appealing, be ready to cut in the best performance and let the discontinuity of the little business ride. You will find that strong performances do what they are supposed to do, engross the audience and involve them more deeply in the story. A minor continuity glitch will most likely not even be noticed when actors are delivering a great performance to the engaged audience.

Be Familiar with All of the Footage

Reviewing and assessing the footage for quality issues and gauging usability at the very beginning of the editing process actually serve a two-fold purpose. Obviously this will help you "pull the selects" or set aside your best shots for use in the assembly edit. It also forces you to become familiar with all of the footage shot for the project. This is exceedingly important because it will be your job to know what options you have during the cutting process. Although not as popular today, capturing from a tape source into your computer allowed you to experience the tapes in real time and you got your first familiarity with the material. If you are working with digital media files copied off a camera's hard drive or memory card, you will still have to watch all of the footage for quality and usability assessment once it is available in your project.

For scripted fictional narrative stories, the script initially guides your approach and the footage may match up for the most part. Use the best material you have when you follow the script's framework. As the editor, though, you are often given the ability to rework scene order and restructure the story a bit differently than what the script called for originally. You are paid for your storytelling abilities, not just as an assembly monkey. If you are working with documentary, news, or even "reality" TV footage, you will have to be rather familiar with everything that is shown (the actions or the **B-roll**) and with everything that is said (interviews and so forth). Adding comments to your clips, embedding markers with script lines or having a timecoded transcript of interviews can all be helpful. You never know which piece of footage will turn a good edit into a great edit. As you begin to frame the story during the edit, the footage itself helps give it form, direction, influence, etc. An editor familiar with all of his or her building blocks can construct a better project.

So How Does All of This Help You?

The job of the editor goes well beyond just slapping together a few pictures and sounds with a song and a title or two. The editor is the person at the end of the creativity chain who takes all of the available assets (all the production footage, graphics, music, etc.) and puts it together in such a way that it makes sense, tells a story, gives information and/or entertains. An editor is a storyteller who also has to possess technical knowledge, not just of the editing tools he or she uses to conduct the edit, but also of film language – the grammar of the shots.

This chapter has presented you with a review of the simple shot types (i.e., long shot, extreme close-up, etc.), what they look like, and how they may be understood by the viewing audience. These basic shots evolve into complex and developing shots as soon as the production team ups the ante and introduces zooms, pans, dolly moves, and so forth. You have also become familiar with a short list of criteria upon which to base your judgments of "good" or "no good" where the footage is concerned. Knowing what not to use in your edited piece is almost as important as knowing what to put in it. Understanding film language and having the ability to scan footage for compromising quality issues are important first steps in becoming a good editor.

Selecting the Best Shots

Chapter Two – Review

1. Coverage provides the editor with different views of the same actions for better choices of showing the scene unfold.

2. The basic shot types are extreme close-up, big close-up / choker, close-up, medium close-up, medium shot, medium long shot, long shot / wide shot, very long shot, extreme long shot, two-shot, and over-the-shoulder shot.

3. Simple shots with only slight subject movement become complex shots when there is a zoom or a pan/tilt action. Complex shots become developing shots when you add camera mount movement as well as more elaborate subject movement.

4. Reviewing your footage for best technical and aesthetic qualities will help you pull your selections for the assemble edit and allow you to be very familiar with all of your video sources.

Chapter Two – Exercises & Projects

1. Watch your favorite movie or TV show and take note of how many CU, MS, LS, OTS and 2-shots occur. Which is used more? At what points in the show do they get used?

2. Develop a very brief scene between two people having a dialogue in any location you wish. Plan the coverage shots for three separate versions; one with simple shots, one with complex shots, and one with developing shots. Edit the footage from each shoot separately. Which cuts together best and why? After comparing each separate sequence take all of the footage from all three shoots and cut a new combined sequence. Do you find it easier to edit a sequence with all three shot categories represented? Yes or No and Why?

Chapter Two – Quiz Yourself

1. Name as many of the basic shot types as you can remember.

2. When and why might you add an extreme long shot to your edited sequence?

3. What information can a close-up convey to an audience?

4. When might it be a good thing to use a blurry shot in a story?

5. You are presented with footage for half of an entire scene that is accidentally amber-toned. The performances are strong but the color does not match the footage from the other half of this scene. Is it totally unusable or might there be something you can do to it or with it in your sequence?

6. True or False: Trimming just a few frames from the tail or head of clips at a continuous action edit may smooth out the illusion of movement across the cut.

7. How would you handle adding 4:3 SD footage into a widescreen 16:9 HD project?

Chapter Three
When to Cut and Why

Factors That Lead to Making an Edit

- Information
- Motivation
- Shot Composition
- Camera Angle
- Continuity
- Sound

Editing a motion picture is more than just assembling a bunch of shots one after the other. It involves the creative placement of various picture and sound elements such that when an audience views the entire piece they will be moved, entertained, informed, or even inspired. This last statement really highlights a fundamental aspect of any motion picture (whether it is a feature film, a TV commercial, a situation comedy, a music video, etc.). The main purpose behind any edited project is for it to be shown to an audience. As an editor, you are tasked with crafting an experience that will affect a viewer in some way – hopefully in a way the producers of the project intend.

The material for the project was written with an audience in mind, the footage was recorded with an audience in mind, and you must edit it together with an audience in mind. And this is not just any audience, but the specific audience that the project is targeting. The same people who would watch a documentary about late nineteenth-century North American textile mills may not see a movie about the pranks at a college fraternity. Understanding audience expectations and their degree of involvement in the program will be an excellent skill to develop during your editing career. Anticipating the needs of the viewer will go a long way toward aiding your approach to editing the material.

Of course, different genres of motion pictures and television programming, etc., may all require different editorial approaches. The unique content and specific target audiences will necessitate the use of different editing styles, techniques, effects, and so forth. As you may be just starting out on your filmmaking journey and your editing career path, you should be watching as many of these motion image products as possible. You will begin to see how they are each treated, the common approaches taken, the presence or lack of certain shared aspects or elements, and so on. Really watching and getting a feel for the work of other editors is a great way to help train your brain. Over time, you will most likely develop a solid interest and rather strong skill set in just one of the programming formats (commercials, documentaries, feature films, news, etc.) and you will spend the majority of your editing career in that genre.

But before we get lost in such specifics about the future job you might have, let us return to the goal of our book, which is to discuss the basic grammar of the edit. Although it is true that different editing jobs will call for different editing techniques, it is also true that there are some common attributes to most styles of editing. These common attributes are the elements that your viewing audience (including yourself) have been trained to expect and comprehend when watching a motion picture. People are rarely conscious of these elements, but, through viewing film and television imagery over their lifetime, they subconsciously know how to "read" certain edits and they can easily decipher meaning in the flow of images across the screen. Just as the basic shot types have meaning in the language of film, how an editor strings those shots together in the motion picture also has meaning to the viewer. There is grammar in the edits.

What Factors Lead to Making an Edit?

In Chapter One we introduced the four major types of transitions that are used at a cut point in a motion picture: cut, dissolve, wipe, and fade. Each one of these transition types enables the editor to move from one shot to the next. We will discuss what may cause an editor to choose from one of these four transition types in the next chapter, but for now, let us explore something even more basic. What factors or elements compel an editor to want to make an edit in the first place? Why cut from one shot to another very particular shot at that very particular moment in time?

The following list is meant to serve as a jumping-off point. These criteria are some of the major reasons for considering a cut when dealing with most material, but, as with many moments in the filmmaking process, other factors not mentioned here might come into play. Using this list will put you in very good shape when editing decisions need to be made.

- Information
- Motivation
- Shot composition
- Camera angle
- Continuity
- Sound

Information

A new shot should always present some new information to the viewer. In a motion picture, this may primarily be visual information (a new character entering a scene, a different location shown, an event whose meaning is not quite known yet, etc.), but it may also be aural (**voice-over narration**, the clatter of horse hooves, a speech, etc.). A smart editor will ask her/himself several questions regarding the "showing" of the story: What *would* the audience like to see next? What *should* the audience see next? What *can't* the audience see next? What do *I wish* for the audience to see next?

One of the many tasks set up for the editor is to engage the audience both emotionally (make them laugh, cry, scream in fright, etc.) and mentally (to make them think, guess, anticipate, etc.). Asking the previous questions can generate clever and inspired ways of showing the same story. In a mystery you may purposefully show misleading information and in a romantic melodrama you may show the audience information that the characters do not yet know. Regardless of the kind of information presented, the fact that it is there to engage the audience, get them involved, and get them thinking helps keep them interested in the motion picture. When audience members are thinking and feeling, they are not paying attention to the physical act of the edit, and this engagement helps keep the movie running strong and smooth. It also means that the editor has done his or her job well.

It must be understood that this element of new information is basic to all editing choices. Whenever one shot has exhausted its information content, then it may be time to cut to another shot. When constructing a scene from a narrative or a segment in a documentary, is there new information in the next shot to be added to your sequence? Is there a better choice? Is there another shot perhaps, from the same scene or from some other source, which does provide new information and fits into the story to make it flow? No matter how beautiful, cool, or expensive a shot may be, if it does not add new information to the progression of the story, then it may not belong in the final edit. It might, however, provide significant tonal value to the scene or the overall mood of the story, and therefore add different sensory information to the audience experience.

FIGURE 3.1 Each shot presented to the audience should provide new information about the story to keep them engaged and attentive. The MLS of the detective cuts to the CU of the nameplate and door buzzer.

Motivation

The new shot you cut to should provide new information, but what about the shot that you are cutting away from? What is the reason to leave that shot? When is a good time to leave the current shot? There should always be a motivation for making a transition away from a shot. This motivation can be either visual or aural or temporal.

PICTURE – In picture terms, the motivating element is often some kind of movement by a subject or an object in the current shot. It could be as big as a car jumping over a river, or as simple as a slight wink of an eye. Perhaps during a close-up a character glances to her left as if looking at something off-screen. Editing logic would hold that you might then want to cut away from her close-up and cut to the object of her interest – what she is looking at in the film space. The motivation to cut away comes from the movement of the actor's eyes and the desire this action initiates in the viewer to see what it is that the character is seeing. A cut to the next shot, of a wolf in Grandma's clothing, provides the audience with new information. It shows them what the woman is looking at, it keeps them informed about the story, and, in this case, it keeps them wondering – *Why is there a guy dressed as a wolf dressed as a grandmother?* (see Figure 3.2).

Another tactic might be that you choose to *not* show the audience what the character is looking at off-screen, but, instead, you cut to some other scene altogether for entirely different information and story progression. Not fulfilling their curiosity keeps the audience wondering, guessing, and in suspense as to what the person was looking at and what happened to that person after we cut away. This approach, of delayed gratification, can work in drama, horror, comedy – just about any genre, provided you eventually return to that initial character and show something that is the "logical" result of what he was looking at earlier in the narrative. The audience will be pleased that you closed the loop on that particular plot point by finally showing them what the object of interest had involved. Either delaying the **reveal** of this information for too long or never answering that question can be a gamble.

SOUND – If you wish to use sound as a motivating element, then you would need to address the editing of both picture and sound tracks more precisely near that transition. The sound that motivates the cut could be generated by something visible in the shot currently on the screen. As an example, a medium long shot (MLS) shows a man standing in a kitchen. A tea kettle, visible on the stove, begins to whistle. The whistle on the soundtrack of the MLS can motivate a cut to a close-up (CU) of the tea kettle on the stovetop. Steam shoots up from the spout and the whistling seems louder (see Figure 3.2). It should be noted that because the close-up shot actually magnifies the visual size and importance of the tea kettle, it can be appropriate to raise the level or volume of the whistle in your audio track as well. This lets the sound produced by that object match the size of the visual object on screen and reflects the "perspective" or proximity of the close-up shot.

Changing this scenario slightly, let us now say that the man is sitting at his dining room table in a medium shot. The tea kettle begins to whistle but the tea kettle, being on the stove in the kitchen, is not visible within this medium shot's composition. You may then cut to the same close-up of the tea kettle that we used in the previous example, again with a louder whistle on the audio track of the new shot. In this case, the audience can recognize and accept this domestic sound even though they do not see the tea kettle. The pay off, and new information, comes when you cut to the close-up of the tea kettle. The audience do not notice the transition from one shot to the next because they are processing the audio information while it leads them into new, and corroborating, visual information. You have motivated an exit from one shot and provided new detailed information in the next shot.

A third and more advanced way of using audio as a transition motivator is rather conceptual in its design. An editor may create what is called a **sound bridge**. A sound, seemingly generated by something not seen or known to the audience, begins under shot one. It motivates the transition into shot two, where the origin of the strange sound is revealed. To modify our tea kettle example slightly, let us say that we are seeing the man in the kitchen with the tea kettle in the MLS. The audience see the steam rise out of the kettle spout and begin to hear what they may interpret as the tea kettle whistling. This motivates the cut to a new shot of an old train's steam engine whistle blowing. The sound of the train whistle, laid under the picture track of the kitchen MLS, acted as a motivator to leave that shot. Then, continuing across the cut, the whistle audio acted as a bridge transitioning the viewer into the new location and new information of shot two. The audience follow the unexpected transition because the new image of the train whistling gives them information to process and gives them a bit of an unexpected surprise which helps keep them engaged in a new line of the story (see Figure 3.2).

TIME – Often an editing choice comes down to the timing. Feeling when to cut may be motivated by the overall pace of the motion picture combined with the rhythm of each particular scene.

The pace of a scene – the duration of each shot on the screen – has a lot to do with the energy of the content, emotion, and purpose of the scene. Is it a dramatic bank robbery gone wrong? Is it a tango-like argument showing unexpected romantic tension between coworkers? Is it a somber scene where a parent must pack up the belongings of her deceased child?

The bank robbery may benefit from quick cutting of different and perhaps odd angles on the scene indicating the confusion, fear, and unpredictable danger brought on by the disruptive and violent act. Both the participants in the scene and the audience are equally disoriented.

The flirtatious argument between unlikely romantic partners may emulate the rhythm of a tango where you cut back and forth and back and forth in equal time – one trying to outdo the other. Perhaps the rhythm quickens, as their argument escalates and the shots get tighter and closer until the characters are united in an "intimate" profile 2-shot, only to cut back out to a wide shot that lasts longer on screen to show them regain their composure and walk away in separate directions.

The grieving parent may be shown in wide shots of very long duration to indicate how still time is now that her child is gone and how isolated she feels lost in this new world, sad and alone. Perhaps the few transitions in the scene are **elliptical** in nature (moving forward in time), showing the mother in different stages of grief while handling different objects in her child's room – as the lighting from the window changes to show passage of time. Here, "film time" – different from real time – is absolutely under the control of the editor.

The pacing of your overall motion picture can be much like a traditional roller coaster. There could be slow scenes, moderate scenes, and fast scenes combined together at different moments of the story's progression. Like on a coaster, in order to go fast you must first go slow – a long, slow ride up the first big hill, then a fast race down, then some little bumps, then a big hill with an unexpected turn, then racing down again and finally a few minor bumps and it's all over before you know it. If it's all too slow, it may feel like you are not going anywhere and become uninteresting. If it's all too fast, it may just become an annoying sensory overload without any breaks. Again, the pacing decisions can be motivated by genre, content, and intent, but varying the pace can give the audience a more engaging ride.

Shot Composition

Traditionally, the film editor could not significantly alter the composition of visual elements in the footage that he or she was given to edit. The relatively high resolution of 35 mm film negative did allow for a certain amount of blow-up or frame enlargement. Standard Definition NTSC video (720 x 486) fell apart rather quickly when you tried to scale the frame. HD (1920 x 1080), being a slightly higher resolution, will allow for some blow-up and re-composition. It is only now, with high-end digital video imagers that can achieve an effective 5K image resolution, that more substantial and

FIGURE 3.2 (A–B) Motivation for the cut comes from the movement of the woman's eyes and the audience's desire to see what she sees. (C–D) Motivation for the cut comes from the audio track of the tea kettle whistling. (E–F) Motivation of the cut to new information, new location comes from the sound bridge of the train whistle beginning under shot one and carrying the viewer along into shot two. (G) How this sound bridge might look in your video editing timeline.

sometimes requisite reframing can be done. However, none of these scaling options for the frame can significantly reposition subjects or objects within the depth (3D space) of the film space of the shots – that was the job of the director and DP during production.

The editor *can* certainly choose what two shots get cut together at a transition. Provided the correct composition is in the visual material, the editor can help make the viewing of these images more engaging for the audience member.

The easiest or most straightforward option for an editor's choice can be to simply edit in all the footage from one, long, beautifully composed shot — be it simple, complex, or developing. The beautiful, well-balanced shot was designed by the filmmakers to be a showpiece, it looks great and plays well once cut into the sequence. The audience is given the time to appreciate the shot for what it is as it unfolds in its entirety. Everybody is happy. Although do not be afraid to cut into this showpiece if the pacing, story, or characterizations can benefit from an added visual interruption.

Another simple technique is to take two basic but properly composed shots and transition them one after the other. A two-person dialogue presents the perfect scenario to demonstrate this. Your scene starts with a wide shot of two people sitting across the table from one another having a discussion. As character A speaks you cut to a close-up of character A. He is sitting frame left with his look room opening across to frame right. Audiences have grown to expect that you will cut over to character B listening in a matching close-up. She is sitting over on frame right with her look room opening across to frame left.

Using the alternating placement of characters frame left and frame right generates interest in the audience members and causes them to stay engaged with the progression of the motion picture. As you cut from CU to CU, the audience is getting to experience eye-line match or eye trace across the screen and across the cuts.

When the viewers are watching character A speak over on frame left, their attention is over on frame left. They are aware, however, that character A's attention is actually across the screen over on frame right. When the cut to character B comes, the audience traces character A's eye-line across the empty screen and rests upon the new face of character B over on frame right. The compositional placement of character B should be in such a place as to match the eye-line from character A, so the audience is rewarded for following the eye trace across the screen and across the edit.

Like a tennis ball bouncing back and forth across the court, the eyes of the viewing audience will travel back and forth across the screen seeking the new information from each character as you cut from one shot composition to the other. You want to engage the audience's eye trace without making them search too hard for the next bit of information. Subtle searches will keep the viewing experience interesting, and more elaborate searches can make it more surprising. Complex and multi-layered shot compositions can look great on screen, but be aware of how you cut into and out of them. Think of how the audience will locate the new, important visual information within the more complex arrangements of on-screen elements.

What Factors Lead to Making an Edit?

FIGURE 3.3 Even traditional compositions like these engage the viewers by asking them to trace the matching eye-line across the empty look room on screen.

Camera Angle

In Chapter Two, we discussed how to review your footage and watch for shots that may have been taken from two positions on set less than 30 degrees apart around the 180 degree arc of the action line. This is one of the key elements of a shot that will help you determine if it should be cut next to another shot from the same coverage. There has to be reasonable difference in the camera angle on action for two shots to be "comfortably" edited together.

When the coverage is planned for a scene, certain camera placements or camera angles are considered to be the most advantageous, and they are the shots eventually recorded by the filmmakers. Due to factors of time and money, only certain shot types from certain angles will be recorded and the production team tries to fit the most information into the fewest, but best looking, shots that they can. But an editor will never know from where around the 180 degree arc the camera was placed to record the actions of the scene until he or she reviews the footage. The editor can only do his or her best to place shots of differing horizontal angles (greater than 30 degrees apart) next to one another in the edit – particularly with dialogue scenes covered in the traditional Master Scene method.

The reason for this is simple. If two shots are recorded with similar framing from two, very near angles on action, then their resulting images will look too similar to one another, even though they are slightly different. This similarity will register with the viewer as he or she watches the program and it may appear to the eye as if there is a glitch or a **jump** in the image at the cut point.

The expression, **jump cut**, is used frequently in the analysis of editing for motion pictures. In this case, as in most, it simply refers to the fact that while watching the motion images, the viewer perceives a jump, a glitch, or an extremely brief interruption or alteration to the pictures being shown. In our current example of these clean single shots with angles on action that are too close, we will find that the images of shot one and shot two are too similar in their appearance (see Figure 3.4). The audience will not see them as providing sufficiently different views on the same information. The image in their eyes will merely jump, which they will consciously notice, and as a result it will pull them out of the viewing experience, which is something that the editor should try to prevent if such a treatment is not part of the project's established visual style. Jump cuts have become popularized in recent times via music videos, film trailers and with certain feature film directors, but that does not mean that they are always excusable.

FIGURE 3.4 Editing together two shots of similar camera angles will cause a jump at the cut point. Differing camera angles and framing will help prevent the "jump cut" in the mind of the viewer.

Continuity

In traditional editing methodologies, providing smooth, seamless **continuity** across transitions is a very important element to keeping edits unnoticed by the viewer. This is called continuity editing or invisible editing. The story is supposed to move forward, uninterrupted, where the shots of differing magnification (LS, MS, CU, etc.) flow from one to the next as if presenting continuous events. Experimental films, and the French Nouvelle Vague (or New Wave) movement of the early 1960s, established that visual continuity (as discussed below) was not absolutely required. Today many filmmakers disregard the strictness of continuity concerns in favor of best performance editing. Jump cuts, time shifts, repeated and alternate action and line delivery have become part of an accepted style of editing and storytelling. Starting with the traditional continuity style, however, is a good place to learn the basic approach to story editing.

Once again, editors are not responsible for the quality of the footage that they are given, but they are responsible for assembling that material into the best motion picture possible. If the production team and talent did not provide visual material with compositional or performance-based continuity, it will be the editor's job to make up for that deficiency in some way in the editing. And to make matters more interesting, there are actually several different forms of continuity that need to be addressed at various points throughout the editing process. Let us take a look.

Continuity of Content

Actions performed by the on-camera talent should ideally match from one shot to the next. Because actors are obliged to perform the same actions take after take, for each shot covered in the scene, one hopes that the overlapping actions were consistent. This is not necessarily always the case. The continuity of content should be watched for but may not be so easily fixed.

As an example, if the family dog is sitting in a chair during the wide shot of a dinner table scene, then the dog should also be seen in the tighter shots used to show the remainder of the scene. If the dog had been taken off set and there were no other shots with the dog sitting at the table with the family, then, as the editor, you get to make a choice. Do you begin the family dinner scene without the wide establishing shot that shows the dog? Perhaps you start the scene on a close-up of the character speaking the first line. Perhaps you start with a close-up of a plate of food, then move out to a two- or three-shot. Additionally, you have the option of showing the dog in the wide shot and then laying in the sound effect of the dog walking away on the hard-wood or linoleum flooring while you show the tighter shots of the family without the dog at the table. Perhaps you cut in a shot of the dog lying on the floor in a different part of the house. Regardless of your approach, you are searching for a solution to a continuity problem.

If a man picks up a telephone in an MLS using his right hand, then the telephone should still be in his right hand when you next transition into an MCU of him speaking on the phone. If, for whatever reason, the production team did not provide any shots of the man with the phone in his right hand, but only in his left, then you could **cut away** to some other shot after the MLS and before the phone-in-left-hand MCU. This will give the audience enough of a break from continuous action so that they can either forget which hand the phone was in, or believe the man had time to transfer the telephone from his right hand to his left while he was off screen. In this case, the cut-away is any brief shot that will provide the appropriate distraction and time filler to allow the audience to make the leap in logic of object continuity adjustment (see Figure 3.5).

So either the footage already contains the proper material to edit with the correct continuity of content, or the editor must create some means of hiding, masking, or "explaining" the visual incongruity. If the audience can be "tricked" into seeing something else, or if the performance presented is so strong, then the questionable content will most likely be overlooked. No matter the approach taken, the editor is like a sleight-of-hand magician purposefully distracting the eyes of the audience to cover the glitch in the picture.

Continuity of Movement

Screen direction is the movement of subjects or objects toward the edges of frame. This should be maintained as you transition from one shot to the next, if that following shot still covers the same movement of the same subjects or objects. The production team should have respected the scene's screen direction and the 180 degree rule during the shooting of coverage. If they did not, and the new shot that you would like to use continues your talent's movement contrary to the established screen direction, then you may have to **insert** a neutral shot that will continue the narrative and still provide a visual break from the discontinuity of movement. This other "inserted" shot, of whatever material you have that fits the narrative flow, will offer the audience a visual break

FIGURE 3.5   Using a cut-away shot may provide the needed break from inconsistent content so that the audience does not consciously notice the discontinuity of the telephone in the man's hand.

that allows the character time to reverse his direction in the third shot continuing the previous action (see Figure 3.6).

Continuity of Position

The film space itself has direction and also a sense of place. Subjects or physical objects within the shot occupy a certain space within the film world as well. It is important for the editor to string together shots where that subject or object placement is maintained continuously. If an actor is shown frame right in shot one, then he should be somewhere on frame right in any subsequent shots during that scene. Of course, if the actor physically moves during the shot to a different location within the film space, then it is logical to show him on a new side of the frame. Cutting together two shots that cause the subject or object to jump from one side of the screen to the other will distract the viewer and the illusion of "invisible" editing will be broken (see Figure 3.7).

FIGURE 3.6 Talent movement should maintain screen direction across the edit point. If you wish to cut together two shots that reverse screen direction, then it may be advisable to use an insert shot to break the audience's attention on the direction of movement.

FIGURE 3.7 The physical position of objects within the film space and the shot composition should stay consistent across edit points. This woman appears to jump from screen right to screen left after the cut to the other character.

Continuity of Sound

The continuity of sound and its perspective is of critical importance to an edited motion picture. If the scene depicts action that is happening in the same place and at the same moments in time, then the sound should continue with relative consistency from one shot to the next. If there is an airplane in the sky in the first shot, and it can be seen and heard by the viewer, then the sound of that airplane should carry over across the transition into the next shot from that scene. Even if the airplane were not seen in the next shot of this sequence, the sound of it would still be audible to the characters; therefore it should still be presented to the audience.

Sound levels for voices and objects should be consistent throughout an edited scene. Changes in object distances from camera, either through shot choices or talent's movements within the film space, should also be accounted for through raising or lowering volume and panning levels in the audio mix for those shots. Perspective/proximity increase or drop off should be represented.

Additionally, all spaces have a background noise level. It may be soft, deep, high, or loud, depending on the environment depicted on screen. This ever-present layer of sound is commonly called **ambience**, but it may also be referred to as **atmosphere** or **natural sound** (**nats** for short). It is responsible for creating a bed of consistent audio tone over which the dialogue and other more prominent sound effects and so forth are placed. This extra, uninterrupted sound bed is either lifted from the production audio recordings (sometimes called **room tone**), or an editor or **sound designer** generates it from other sources. This ambience track adds a mood or feeling and a certain believability to the location of the scene for the audience. Its presence should be regulated in the mix so that it is minimized under dialogue, etc., but may become more prominent when it does not compete with other, more important sounds.

Is There a Right or Wrong Reason for a Cut?

Yes and no. As with anything that involves a craft, there are the technical methods and reasons for doing things certain ways, but then there are the aesthetic or creative reasons for doing other things in other ways. How you make an edit and why you make an edit are two different aspects of the process, but they are always interrelated. You can edit a project as you see fit, but in the end, it will be the viewing audience that decides whether your choices were right or wrong. Did the edits work or not? Did the audience notice them or not? As long as you have reasons why you made each edit, you are on the right path. Keeping the various elements mentioned in this chapter in mind and pre-thinking what your audience would appreciate will keep you thinking about why you choose to edit when you do.

Chapter Three – Review

1. Know your audience and remember that you are really editing a story for them to experience.

2. Each shot you transition into should provide the viewer with new information, or defines a tone or mood that progresses the "story" of the project.

3. Each transition you create should be motivated by some visual or aural element within the shot you are leaving.

4. The timing of the shots in each scene and the overall pacing of the entire motion picture should reflect the energy of the content, mood, and emotional levels of the characters and the development of the story.

5. Juxtaposing appropriately dissimilar shot compositions across the transition leads the viewers' eyes around the frame as they seek new visual information, and therefore keeps them engaged.

6. Present differing camera angles and shot types to the viewers within a given scene or sequence so they will not experience a temporal or spatial jump cut – unless that is a visual style in your project.

7. Ensure, as best as possible, that your transitions conform to the appropriate continuity of content, movement, position, and sound if you are going for the "invisible" edit style.

Chapter Three – Exercises & Projects

1. Watch a scene or section from any motion media project. Get a feeling for the durations of the shots (or frequency of transitions) and see if they remain constant, rise in number, or lower in number.

2. Using the same scene or section, determine what factor(s) led to the edits occurring when they do. Is it information, motivation, composition, angle, continuity, or a combination of several? Is it something entirely separate from these factors?

3. Edit together a brief sequence (maybe ten clips) of any source video that you have available. It helps if the material is of all different subject matter. When you edit it together, take notes on what object or portion of the screen you look at just after each cut point. Show this same sequence to a friend or classmate and have them tell you the first thing they look at after each cut. Screen the sequence several more times to other individuals and record their objects of interest or

areas of frame that they look at. Compare what you, the editor, chose to look at in each new clip with the responses of your selected viewers. Do they match? Is there a trend? Are they all different? What might these results mean?

4. Create a quick scenario where a sound bridge across the cut could be applied. You only need two shots – the end of one segment A and the beginning of the next segment B. Cut two versions of the transition: one with a straight cut from A to B; a second with the same straight cut but with your bridging sound clip across the cut underneath both the end of A and the start of B. Play the two versions back to back. Which do you prefer? Which do others prefer?

Chapter Three – Quiz Yourself

1. You are given four shots: 1. WS – high school cafeteria 2. ECU of mobile phone text message saying "Duck" 3. MS of a boy being hit by a volley of green peas 4. CU of same boy looking off screen at something. In what order would you edit these four clips and what factors play into your decisions?

2. What significance does the shot composition have when you cut from one shot to the next? How can these compositions engage the audience?

3. How can a mismatch in screen direction or screen position from two different coverage shots challenge an editor cutting a dialogue scene?

4. The sound of an environment or location within a film has several names. List as many of the names as you remember.

5. How can the pacing of a motion picture be like an amusement park ride?

Chapter Four
Transitions and Edit Categories

- The Cut
- The Dissolve
- The Wipe
- The Fade
- The Action Edit
- The Screen Position Edit
- The Form Edit
- The Concept Edit
- The Combined Edit

Now that you are familiar with basic shot types, and with some factors needing your consideration when you wish to make a solid edit, we should really shed some light on the most common types of transitions that you will use at those edit points. As mentioned earlier, we will be discussing the cut, the dissolve, the wipe, and the fade. Each one of these four transitions carries with it its own meaning when viewed within a motion picture project. Audiences understand these transitions and have certain expectations around their traditional use. We will break down each one and analyze how they play into the six elements of information, motivation, composition, camera angle, continuity, and sound.

The Cut

The cut is the most frequently used transition in any kind of filmmaking. It can be defined as an instantaneous change from one image to another. If you are working in the continuity style of "invisible" editing, then the viewing audience should not consciously notice the cut transition. When it is made at the correct moment, following as many of the positive edit elements as possible, it will seem transparent within the flow of space, time, and action. Creatively, however, cuts do not have to be invisible. A hard and abrupt jump from one screen image to another can represent the mood of your story perfectly. Hidden or not, cuts instantly change picture or sound (or both) for the audience.

The term cut stems from the very beginnings of motion picture film history. The actual strip of flexible plastic that contained the images in individual frames was physically cut, either with scissors or with a razor blade splicer. Joining two shorter strips of film together, with either tape or glue, was the easiest, fastest, and cheapest way to make a transition. Hence it was used a great deal. The people who cut filmstrips were called cutters before they were called editors. The expression still holds today even though most people who carry out film and video editing use computer software. An editor can be called a cutter and the act of editing a film can still be called cutting. Over the one hundred years since the origins of cinema, the cut has not changed at all.

The cut is most often used where:

- The action is continuous
- There needs to be a sudden change for visual or aural "impact"
- There is a change in information or location

It is possible to make good cuts and not-so-good cuts. If you consider all six of the following elements when you are making the cut, you are much more likely to help yourself make a good edit (see Figure 4.1).

1. Information – The shot that is currently playing, shot one, has provided the audience with all the visual and aural information that it could provide. The editor then cuts to shot two to provide the audience with new information. Ideally, every shot in a motion picture should offer some form of new information such as an establishing view of a location, a close-up detail of a computer screen, the sound of rain falling or a baby crying, etc.

2. Motivation – There should always be a reason to make the cut. Something within shot one leads to the need to display shot two. It could be just a need to show new information. It could be a large action within the frame. It could be as small as an actor's slight eye movement. Perhaps there is a noise heard from within the film space but off screen. An editor may even determine that pacing, alone, is a good enough reason to motivate the cut.

   The nature of the program and the content of the footage help determine what or when a motivated cut could occur. The timing of shots, clip durations, and frequency of cuts play an important role in motivating edits. These durations of time are generally not marked down in seconds or frames but take on more of a "gut feeling" unit of time known as a **beat**. They create the rhythm of the scene and add to the overall pacing of the entire story. The motivation for the cut's timing could be based on this intangible yet somehow instinctually knowable beat or feeling that it is now time to cut to something different.

3. Composition – Having chosen the end frame of the current shot, you will know what its composition looks like. A good edit will have the next shot display a different composition from the first. If the two shots at the instantaneous cut are too similar in their composition, even though they are of totally different subject matter, it can appear as a visual "jump cut" to the audience.

4. Using differences in composition at cut points forces the viewer to immediately engage their eyes and brain and search for the new visual information in the new shot. As long as they are not confused by an overly busy composition in the new shot, they do not even notice the actual cut as they get engrossed in experiencing the visual elements of this shot.

   Camera angle – During the editing of a scene, each successive shot cut into a sequence should show a different camera angle from the previous shot. A clean single or an over-the-shoulder shot recorded somewhere else along the 180-degree arc could immediately follow a medium long shot of two people talking in profile. Focal length changes may also be considered useful in new shot choices for this scene, but a cut would require an angle change to be most effective.

   If the camera does not shift in its horizontal angle, but is either zoomed in or moved closer to the subjects on the same lens axis, then a tighter shot is created with the same angle on the same subjects. In our written example above, **punching-in** to a tight medium two shot from the same angle as the medium long shot of the two characters in profile may not be a good choice. This is

The Cut

sometimes called a **cut-in** or an **axial edit**. The lack of significant difference in angle on action may result in a jump cut.

5. Continuity – The continuous movement or action should be both evident and well matched in the two shots to be cut together. The cut is instantaneous, so the fluid movement should be maintained across the cut. Human viewers are extremely attuned to discontinuities in action across cuts and they are easily detected and disliked.

6. Sound – There should ideally be some form of sound continuity or sound development across the cut point. If a cut happens within footage from the same scene and location, then the ambience should carry over across the cut. Audio levels should match the visuals' perspective on the screen for each shot at the cut point. If you cut dramatically from one location or time to another, then immediate differences in sound type and volume can be useful to highlight the shift in space, time, or feeling. These are sometimes called **smash cuts** (and could also apply to abrupt visual changes at the cut). Otherwise, a gradual shift might be preferred where L-cuts help smooth over the transition change.

In a perfect world, each cut would contain strong aspects of each of the above elements, but that scenario may not always be achievable. Your goal should be to watch for these elements in all of your footage, train your eyes and ears to pick up on them, and use them as appropriate during your edit process. You should always use "the cut" when creating your **assemble edit** (what some people call the **slop edit** due to how quickly you are able to just slop the selected takes together). It is the default edit tool of editing software and it is the fastest way to work. When trimmed as necessary, each cut in your final sequence should be unnoticed by anyone who watches the show if you are using an "invisible" continuity style of editing. Straight cuts are widely accepted when they work and wildly distracting when they do not (did somebody say jump cuts?). Develop your editing skill set around solid cuts and you will never go wrong. Play too much with the grammar of the cut and you may run into too many problems with your work.

FIGURE 4.1 (A–B) A cut can unite two shots that represent continuous action. (C–D) A cut may end a sequence and lead the viewer into a new location.

The Dissolve

This is the second most common transition used in motion pictures, and, unlike most straight cuts, it attracts attention to itself on purpose. As you may recall from Chapter One, the dissolve is defined as a gradual change from the ending pictures of one shot into the beginning pictures of the next shot. This is traditionally achieved via a superimposition of both shots with a simultaneous downward and upward ramping of opacity (visibility) over a particular period of time. As the end of the first shot "dissolves" away, the beginning of the next shot emerges onto the screen underneath it at the same time. You get to see the images overlapping. A dissolve may also be referred to as a "lap dissolve," a "lap," and sometimes a video "mix." The standard default duration of dissolves in editing software is one second, but this can be easily changed to the length required by the given variables at that particular dissolving point in the story.

The dissolve is most often used where:

- There is a change in time
- There is a change in location
- Time needs to be slowed down or sped up
- There is an emotional component to the subject in the story
- There is a strong visual relationship between the outgoing and the incoming images

A good dissolve is achieved when as many as possible of the following elements are addressed at the point of transition:

1. Information – Much like a straight cut, the new shot should contain new information for the viewer to digest. Whether the dissolve is condensing time over a long, continuous event, changing time periods or locations, or joining disparate concepts through matching imagery, the second shot into which you are dissolving should offer something new to both the viewer and to the narrative of the motion picture.

2. Motivation – As with all transitions, there should be a precise motivating action or narrative need to apply a dissolve. This could be moving backwards or forwards through time, or into or out of states of consciousness. Because dissolves happen across certain durations, they are usually associated with slowing the rhythm of a scene.

3. Composition – The two shots dissolving together should each have compositions that overlap easily and avoid a visual "mess" – particularly at the midpoint when both images are, typically, at 50% opacity. You may dissolve opposing compositional frames (shot one has its subject frame left while shot two has its subject frame right) to unify the images in one, momentary yet well-balanced dissolving frame.

   You may also create a **match dissolve** where the compositions of the two shots are very similar but they have different subject matter. Consider the following example – the scene involves a man who is a werewolf; as he begins to twitch and snarl you cut to an XCU of his bloodshot eyeball with pupil dilating rapidly, then DISSOLVE TO a close-up of the full moon. The two round objects match in composition and shape as the dissolve momentarily joins these images for the audience.

4. Camera angle – Generally you will dissolve between two shots that present differing camera angles on the action, either from footage within the same scene or from two adjacent scenes in the story. Sometimes you may need to collapse time for one long, continuous event recorded from the same angle. Consider the following example – a bank robber is "trapped" in his hideout waiting for his partner to arrive. The scene encompasses time from late afternoon to late evening with appropriate lighting changes throughout. It is all shot from only one stationary camera angle. To compress time, and quickly show the escalating agitation of the man, the editor dissolves between short portions of footage. From daylight through drawn shades to dim desk lamp, the audience gets to watch the character move around the room, sit down, lie down, check his phone, peek out the window, etc. – all over elapsed "film time" via these multiple dissolves.

5. Sound – It is customary to also mix together the audio tracks of the two shots being dissolved in what is often called an audio **cross fade**. As the picture for shot one is dissolving away gradually under the incoming image of shot two, the audio tracks for shot one are also fading down (growing quieter) while the audio for shot two is fading up (growing louder).

6. Time – An important element in the efficacy of the dissolve is its duration, or how long it lingers on screen. One second is usually the default duration for dissolves in video editing software, but a dissolve can last for as long as there is visual material in each shot involved in the transition. In general, the dissolve should last as long as is required for its purpose in the motion picture. A quick dissolve

The Dissolve

of just a few overlapping frames, sometimes referred to as a "soft cut," might be preferable to an instantaneous straight cut – but beware that this can imitate a jump cut. A long dissolve can be on screen for several seconds and may, along the midpoint of this longer duration, appear more like a **superimposition** of the two shots rather than a dissolve. If the story calls for such a visual treatment of these two images uniting for this longer period, then so be it.

The dissolve allows the editor to play with time. If you were editing a story that involved a **flashback**, you could dissolve from the last shot of the present time to the first shot of the events from the past. Also, the dissolve is often used to create a **montage** of many different images that condenses events over time; for example, a day at the amusement park is shown through ten shots that dissolve from one to the next, the whole sequence lasting only thirty seconds of screen time. Usually such special treatments of visual material are planned by the filmmakers from the outset of the project, but editors should feel free to experiment with dissolving time if they find certain scenes to be too long.

It is important to note that dissolves can also slow down time and manipulate the emotions of an audience when accompanied by **slow motion** imagery. A romantic or maybe an emotionally sad sequence can use dissolves rather effectively to slow down events and give the audience time to view and digest the meaning of the material. The gradual transition from image to image softens the experience. It is said that dissolves are the "tear jerker" transition. They allow the viewer time to think and feel, they are associated with more languid, somber, or "thoughtful" emotional responses to the visual story elements.

Dissolves can be used in any time-based motion media piece such as fictional narrative movies, television shows, music videos, documentaries, animated cartoons, how-to and wedding videos, and so forth. There was a time that you would have been hard pressed to find dissolves in the daily news, but even factual reporting has incorporated the "manipulative" transition. An indication of how the rules of visual grammar are changing with our never-ending 24-hour mobile access to motion media.

FIGURE 4.2 Frames that represent a dissolve from one shot to another.

The Wipe

The wipe may be thought of as a cross between a cut and a dissolve. It has a duration like a dissolve but it tends to be performed very quickly. You get to see both images on the screen at once, as in a dissolve, but there is usually no superimposition involved. Wipes are meant to be noticed by the audience and often appear as shapes, or with other graphic elements associated with them. Wipes can zigzag, iris, or spiral, and move diagonally, horizontally, or vertically across the screen, replacing the previous shot with a new shot.

The wipe is most often used where:

- There is a change in time
- There is a change in location
- There is NO strong visual relationship between the outgoing and the incoming images
- Projects call for more visually graphical and engaging treatments at transitions

A good wipe, often a highly stylized transition effect, does not always have to follow the standard elements that lead to good edits:

1. Information – Certainly the shot wiping on the screen will provide the viewing audience with new information, but it need not be related to the shot leaving the screen.

2. Motivation – The simple need for an editor to leave one location or one segment of a program can be enough motivation for the use of a wipe. The movement of an object in the outgoing shot may also provide motivation for a certain shape, timing or direction for a wipe effect. Sometimes, if you have no purposeful way of getting from one place, time, or topic to another, you can use a creative wipe to "entertain" the viewer across the duration of the transition and lead them to a totally new time, place, or topic. Within the grammar of editing transitions, the wipe is the most fanciful way of moving around time and space. If the motivation for the edit transition is to quicken the pace, then fast wipes are a fun and stylized way to achieve this speed of changing the visual elements of the motion picture.

3. Composition – With careful planning, a clever filmmaker may conceive of strong vertical or horizontal movements within the shot composition and the clever

editor will turn these visual elements into what are called **natural wipes**. Objects within the action of the **outgoing** picture frames appear to push or pull or in some way "wipe" across the screen, which allows for a cut or a wipe to the next **incoming** shot. Because there will be portions of two shots on screen, it can be beneficial to have the compositions match, mirror, or balance one another in some way during the wiping process. You may also find that the style or shape of the wiping element is an interesting graphical composition in itself, and the framing of the shots just ending and just beginning around the wipe do not require any special visual connection.

4. Camera angle – Much like the freedom found in the types of compositions around the wipe, there is no real need to adhere to the differing camera angle rules here. The wipe serves to literally wipe the slate clean from the previous shot and introduce a new deal – camera angles are beside the point, but still feel free to creatively explore your options.

5. Sound – Depending on the type or style of wipe you choose to use, sound can be treated as a straight cut, L-cut, or a cross fade at the transition. Sound may lead the wiping shot or follow after it. One has a great deal of freedom in playing with how the audio behaves during the wipe. Depending on the type of program being edited, it is often appropriate to give the wipe action its own sound effect, such as a "**swoosh**."

6. Time – Just as dissolves happen across time, wipes need to have durations as well. Fast wipes can transition quickly from one shot to the next when the tempo of the edited piece necessitates moving the story along. If the edited show calls for slower, more lingering wipes, then they could last for a second or more, although this may get tedious for a viewer. Fast and fun is generally the way to go.

The graphical wipe often acts as a fun distraction, or a way to bridge two disparate and otherwise not easily joined segments of a program. In classical Hollywood cinema of the 1930s they were a fanciful, more graphically pleasing way to transition from one place or time to another. They take the place of the more mundane dissolves. They have more pep. In today's visual marketplace, wipes can take on any shape or form and are appropriate to use in most genres, but are popular in comedy, fantasy, sci-fi, and children's programming, and less so in straight drama.

The Wipe

FIGURE 4.3 The wipe literally wipes one image off the screen and replaces it with a new one. They may be used as fast and fun transitions from any shot to any other shot.

The Fade

Motion pictures or sequences from television programs traditionally begin and end with a fade. If you have ever written or read a screenplay, you most likely saw that the first line may have been **fade in** and the last line was **fade out**. This means that, as a fade in (sometimes called a **fade up**), the screen starts out entirely black and then gradually the black fades away to reveal a fully visible image underneath it signaling that the story has begun. As a fade out (sometimes called a **fade down**), the images at the end of your show gradually fade into a fully opaque black screen signaling that the story has ended. Fades can take on any color, but most often you will see black and occasionally white.

The fade in is most often used:

- At the beginning of a program
- At the beginning of a chapter, scene, sequence, or act
- Where there is a change in time
- Where there is a change in location

The fade out is most often used:

- At the end of a program
- At the end of a chapter, scene, sequence, or act
- Where there is a change in time
- Where there is a change in location

For a fade to be most effective, it should address the following elements:

1. Motivation – The fact that the motion picture is beginning motivates the use of a fade in, and when you have reached the end of a segment or act, it is acceptable to fade out. That is motivation enough for the fade. A fade in abutting a fade out at the cut point is often called a "dip to black" or a "kissing black" and serves as a motivation to slow the pacing between segments – like a long, slow blink.

2. Composition – It can be very helpful in achieving a clean fade in or fade out to use shots that will either begin or end (or both) with a low **contrast** image. Compositionally speaking, you would not wish to have prominent areas of dark and light within the frame, because as the opacity gradually fills in the image or takes it away toward black, the discrepancy between the heavily light and dark areas of the frame will create an imbalance in brightness and make the fading action appear uneven or poorly timed.

The Fade

3. Sound – It is traditional to have the sound levels rise up under the brightening picture of the fade in. The audio should also fade down as the picture exhibits the fade to black or fade out at the end. If a fade out from one scene lingers on the all-black screen, it is often acceptable to fade up the new audio of the yet to be seen next segment before the fade in occurs. This is an example of sound leading picture.

4. Time – Like dissolves and wipes, the fade requires an appropriate duration. Depending on the project, it could last anywhere from one-half second to several seconds. Usually you will just feel what the right amount of time is because staring at an all-black screen for too long, without any new information on the audio track, will feel off-putting. This is a good example of when you should listen to your gut and feel the right "beats" for appropriate timing.

Fades in and out have long been part of film language and a standard tool of the editor when starting or ending any motion picture project. They act as transitions into and out of the dream-like state that is motion picture viewing.

FIGURE 4.4 The fade out ends one sequence and leads the viewer to new material as it transitions into a fade in on the first shot of the next sequence.

As a technical note, all transitions except for "the cut" and some fades require the existence of extra frames of media for the outgoing shot and the incoming shot so that they
may overlap during the transition. The end of Shot 1, referred to as the **tail**, shows
a particular frame just prior to the cut. In order for a dissolve or wipe to occur, there
must be more frames of video in the original master clip that come after the visible
tail frame of Shot 1 in the sequence. The same should hold true for Shot 2. Its first visible frame after the cut, called the **head** frame of that clip segment, must have video
frames that precede it in its master clip. These extra frames of video (and maybe audio)
that are accessed from the master clip are used by the editing software to make the
dissolving or wiping transition effect in your sequence. If your original media does not
have these extra frames (often called head or tail "**handles**") then you will not be able
to create that transition effect of that duration with that positioning across the cut.
As an example, if you are editing an NTSC 30 fps video sequence and you wish to add a
default one second, centered-on-cut dissolve at an edit point in your timeline, then the
software will "borrow" 15 frames from the tail handle of Shot 1 (for after the cut) and
15 frames from the head handle of Shot 2 (for just prior to the cut). In total, 30 frames
of outgoing and incoming video will be dissolved across the edit point.

The Fade

The Five Major Categories of Edit Types

So far we have explored three categories of shot types, eleven kinds of basic shots, six elements that help make a good edit possible, and four major transitions. Now we are going to examine five categories of edit types that touch on most of the major kinds of edits that can be performed with most material. Granted, the type of project you are editing will help decide which kinds of edits you will be able to execute. Certain genres call for certain editorial treatments, but most programs could be completed using one or more of these edit categories.

Our five categories for the different types of edit are:

- Action edit
- Screen position edit
- Form edit
- Concept edit
- Combined edit

In Chapter Three, it was discussed how all edits can benefit from possessing attributes or addressing conditions found in the list of six elements that make edits stronger. The five categories listed above are all different types of edits, therefore it would hold that each type of edit should also benefit from the same six elements. Let us examine each one and provide some examples.

The Action Edit

The **action edit** is nearly always a straight cut. As its name implies, this category encompasses edits between shots that depict continuous action or movement of subjects or objects. As a result, this type of edit may also be called a movement edit or a continuity edit. The first shot in the series will show: a person performing an action – cut point – then the second shot continuing that action but with a different shot type. Time is unbroken. Movements appear to be smooth and continuous across the cut.

As a simple example, in a long shot we see a woman sitting at a cafe table. She lifts a book closer to her head to read it. CUT. After the cut we see the woman in a close-up holding the book so we can read the title on the cover and watch her eyes scan the pages rapidly (see Figure 4.5).

1. Information – The long shot provides the audience with important information about the location, the subject, and the time of day, how the woman is dressed, and what her actions are like — slow, quick, normal, or abnormal. The new CU shot shows the book title.
2. Motivation – In the long shot, the woman will pick up the book off the cafe table and raise it closer to her face. The action of lifting the book will be a good place to make the cut. The action is the motivator, using the placement of the book, over the woman's face, to motivate a cut in to the close-up of the book's title and the woman's eyes.
3. Composition – The arrangements of subject, objects, and set dressing within the frame of the long shot create a strong diagonal exterior space. There are **foreground**, **middle ground**, and **background** layers. The close-up shot offers a centrally weighted frame with the details of the book taking up most of the space. Although framing the woman toward the right may have been more in line

FIGURE 4.5 The motion of raising the book to read it motivates the cut on this action edit.

with her placement in the wider shot, the title of the book and the appearance of the woman's eyes are the most important thing in this new shot, so the centralized framing is working better for the "showing" of narrative information in this case.

4. Camera angle – In the long shot, the camera angle is on a three-quarter profile of the woman's left cheek. In the close-up, the camera has moved around the arc and approaches her face from a much more frontal framing. The difference between the camera angles of these two shots is more than adequate for the cut.

5. Continuity – The most important aspect of the action edit is the continuity, and the continuity of movement really should match at this cut point – hence the use of related terms "match cut" and "matching action." The coverage in the long shot does provide the action of the woman raising the book from the table and opening it in front of her face. The close-up repeats that same overlapping action of the book raised and open, plus it continues along with the woman's eye movements across the pages. As the editor of this action edit, you would be free to cut and match the movement of the book at any point during the action. Because you cut on action, the audience is less likely to perceive the cut, and merely register the presentation of new information about the book and about the woman's eyes.

6. Sound – Because this is a street scene, the ambient sounds could be rather varied. There should always be some sounds associated with the background of the location; perhaps a "bus drive-by" or a "car horn honking" here and there, plus the "chirping" of birds, etc. You could even address the sound of the book being picked up or the pages turning once you move in to the close-up shot. The sound bed should match across the cut.

The action edit is quite common and can be used in very elaborate action hero chase scenes or in very quiet, slow-moving melodramas. As long as there is a continuous action or movement in the frame, the editor can use that to match the same action from another coverage shot from the scene. Some recommend a one-third/ two-thirds approach, where you cut away from Shot 1 at a point where the action is one-third complete and cut into Shot 2 when the matching action has two-thirds remaining. In practice, you are free to cut anywhere along the action that makes the edit work. If the cut addresses the six elements listed above, it should be smooth, unobtrusive, and allow an uninterrupted visual flow for the story unfolding on the screen.

The Screen Position Edit

This type of edit is sometimes called a directional edit or a placement edit. "Directional" because the edit helps direct the viewer's eyes around the screen, and "placement" because it is the unique placement of subjects or objects in the two shots cut together that make the viewer's eyes move around the frame. The screen position edit can be a cut, a dissolve, or even a wipe, but it is usually a cut if there is no passage of time implied by the edit.

The way the shots of a scene are originally conceived (through storyboards or script notes), composed, and recorded will help an editor to construct a screen position edit. Two shots in the coverage were designed to lead the audience's eyes around the screen. Usually one strong visual element occupies one side of the frame and casts its attention, movement or line toward the other side of the frame. Cutting to the new shot, the object of attention is usually shown on the opposite side, fulfilling the viewer's need to see something occupy that visual space. The goal is to engage the audience physically (eye movement around the screen image), mentally (seeking and finding new visual information about characters and the plot), and emotionally (what you draw their eye to in the new shot may be cute, horrific, breathtaking, etc.).

Serving as a basic example of a screen position edit is the traditional two-person dialogue scene shot with Master Scene technique. Beginning with a medium long shot, two people, in profile to camera, face one another and have a conversation. The standard coverage would call for solo medium shots and maybe medium close-ups of each of the two characters. When it comes time to edit, you could go from the wider two-shot into the solo medium close-up shot of character A who is shown frame left. While speaking, his gaze is directed toward frame right. You cut to a medium close-up shot of character B who is shown frame right (see Figure 4.6).

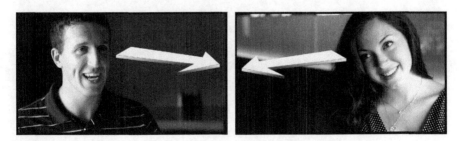

FIGURE 4.6   The screen position edit in its most basic form. One subject is frame left while the other occupies space over on frame right in the next shot. The eyes of the audience are directed across the screen at the edit point following the sight lines.

The Five Major Categories of Edit Types

The new, closer shot of character B yields new information for the audience. Any gesture by character A, or even the line of dialogue being uttered, would be a motivator for the cut. The mirrored **composition** is truly the linkage to the screen position category. The audience had their eyes over on frame left for character A and then had to move them across the screen at the cut point to observe character B in the new shot. The camera angles around the shooting arc are significantly different. Continuity of dialogue delivery is met by the cut, which also means the sound is continuous as well. Not every screen position edit will address all six of the edit elements, but the more the merrier.

The Form Edit

The form edit is best described as a transition from a shot that has a pronounced shape, color, or dimensional composition, to another shot that has a similar shape, color, or dimensional composition. These types of edits are usually preconceived during the writing or pre-production phase because the visual elements that will match require the correct treatment of composition and, sometimes, screen direction. Rarely is the form edit just blind luck on the part of the editor but it can happen, so watch for the opportunity in the visual material. They are sometimes called **graphic edits**.

If using sound as the motivation, the form edit can be a straight cut, but in most cases, the transition will be a dissolve. This is particularly true when there is a change of location and/or perhaps a change in time from one shot to the next. The term **match dissolve** is often used to describe this type of form edit. Our werewolf/full-moon dissolve mentioned earlier is a good example.

A simple scenario will serve to demonstrate a form edit. In a story about a man returning to his small rural village, a series of close-up shots were taken of a jet plane tire, a car tire, a bicycle tire, and a wagon wheel all spinning counterclockwise as they travel over the ground. The four round shapes are framed roughly the same size with a central placement in the shot composition. Essentially they all match. As the editor, if your goal is to condense the man's travel time, you could dissolve from one tire shot into the next until you end up with the close-up of the wagon wheel. You could then cut to a shot of the man sitting among some goats and dried corn stalks in the back of a mule-drawn wagon (see Figure 4.7).

The audience will understand that the dissolving transitions are condensing time. The technological de-evolution of the wheel shapes will show the audience that the man is moving further into the rural area of his home village. The consistency of shape and composition helps keep the viewer's eye trained on the center of the screen and allows the viewer the focus needed to understand the meaning. The sound elements will also digress from very loud to rather quiet as they cross-fade into one another under the corresponding dissolving pictures, supporting the audience's sense of location change. Music under this mini-montage could also be appropriate.

Form edits are also often used in advertising and television commercials. In thirty seconds it can be difficult to say your message concisely, so most often advertisers try to show their message in more easily understood graphical ways. Take, for instance,

FIGURE 4.7   The form edit of the wheels dissolving quickly takes the audience to new locations.

a public service announcement for an anti-smoking campaign. The **spot** calls for a studio shot of several cigarette packages standing up on end in a field of endless white. One package is the most prominent standing up in front of all others. During the spot, this shot dissolves into a shot of headstones at a cemetery. Each cigarette package was standing in the exact spot where a grave marker is standing in the second shot (see Figure 4.8).

FIGURE 4.8   The form edit of the packages and the headstones generates a meaning in the mind of the viewer.

An audience may draw a conclusion from this form edit – that smoking cigarettes may lead to an early death. Whatever the perceived message of this PSA, the use of the form edit (match dissolve) is what helps the audience to interpret meaning. The shapes are simple rectangles. The compositions match exactly. The juxtaposition and the "union" of the imagery during the dissolve generate a rather clear meaning and convey the message smoothly and succinctly. Provided the duration of the dissolve for this form edit was long enough, and the audio tracks worked together, the audience would flow easily from one shot into the next thanks to the matching forms.

The Five Major Categories of Edit Types

The Concept Edit

The concept edit may stand alone as a purely mental suggestion. This type of edit is sometimes called a **dynamic edit**, an **idea edit**, an **intellectual edit,** or **intellectual montage**. The concept edit can take two shots of different content and, through the juxtaposition of these visual elements at that particular time in the story, they can generate implied meaning not explicitly told in the story. This type of edit can cover changes in place, time, people, and even in the story itself, and it can do so without any obvious visual break for the viewer.

Most often, the concept edit is planned by the filmmaker from an early stage of picture development. He or she already knows that the two separate shots, when joined together in the narrative at a certain point, will convey a mood, make some dramatic emphasis, or even create an abstract idea in the mind of the viewer. It is rare, but not impossible, for an editor to create a concept edit from footage that was not intended to form a concept edit. Be forewarned, though, that these types of edits can be tricky, and if the intended meaning is not clear to the viewer then you just may contribute to an unwanted interruption of the flow of visual information.

The previous example of the cigarette packs and the gravestones is very much like a concept edit. The idea that smoking may be bad for you stems from the picture of the cigarettes dissolving into the gravestones. Their unification on screen also equates them in the mind of the viewer. Using one may lead to the other.

Another example of a concept edit would be the following scenario. Two couples are out on a date and one woman announces to the group that she and her boyfriend are now engaged to be married. The friend turns to the newly engaged man and asks, "So how does it feel to be getting married?" – CUT TO – close-up of a television screen; an old black and white prison movie is playing and the inmate wears shackles around his ankles – CUT TO – wide shot of engaged man and woman, sitting on a couch watching the movie (see Figure 4.9).

Neither shot has anything to do with the other. The group shot of the couples at the restaurant is, in no way, connected to the close-up shot of the old prison movie. The six elements need not be applied here. It is not the elements in the shots that make the concept edit, but the effect of what happens in the viewer's mind when these two shots are joined together at that time. Clearly the engaged man is having some second thoughts about the concept of marriage.

FIGURE 4.9 The concept edit conjures an idea in the mind of the viewer through the juxtaposition of seemingly unrelated shots.

The Combined Edit

The combined edit can be a difficult edit to come by in edited programming because it requires a good deal of pre-production planning on the part of the filmmaker. It would be rare that two, unplanned, shots could be cut into a combined edit by the editor alone. The combined edit combines two or more of the four other types of edits. One transition may contain an action edit combined with a screen direction edit, and there may be a form edit and concept edit all in one.

Consider a children's fantasy story where young brothers are playing in their pajamas just before bedtime. They are pretending to fight off some goblins with a flashlight and a pillow. One brother tosses the flashlight to the other – CUT TO – a sword landing in the hand of the second brother, now clad in battle armor, standing on a narrow ledge in a cave fighting off real goblins (see Figure 4.10).

If planned well and shot properly, this scenario has many elements that will make it a good candidate for a combined edit. First, the action of tossing the flashlight across the room makes this an action edit. Second, the screen position of the flashlight and sword is similar. Third, the forms of the two objects are similar – the flashlight and the handle of the sword. And lastly, the concept of the power of imagination may be gleaned from this edit. The boys at play actually transition into the heroes of their fantasy.

FIGURE 4.10 The combined edit takes on multiple attributes of several other edit categories.

Does Everything Always Apply?

The job of the editor is not to memorize the six elements of good edits or the five types of edit categories as presented in this book, but to use the reasoning behind these concepts to inform his or her choices while making the edits. Knowing that cuts, dissolves, wipes, and fades are made in different ways, have different meanings, and can convey different experiences to the viewing audience is very important. Joining shots together at a certain time, in a certain way, for those certain reasons is really what your goal should be. Knowing the grammar of the edit will help you to better execute the edit. This, and practice over time, will enable your skills to develop even more.

The Five Major Categories of Edit Types

Chapter Four – Review

1. Straight cuts are great for continuous action, when there needs to be a sudden change for "visual impact," and when there is a change in plot point or location.

2. Dissolves are used to help change time or location, draw out an emotion, or where there is a strong visual relationship between the outgoing and incoming imagery.

3. The wipe can be used to jump in time, jump in location, unite two totally unrelated shots simply to move the "story" along, or just because the project calls for a more graphically engaging transition.

4. The fade in begins a program, scene, or sequence. The fade out ends a program, scene, or sequence.

5. Action edits join shots that cover continuous, uninterrupted action or movement.

6. Screen position edits, through well-planned shot composition, purposefully draw the audience's attention from one section of the screen to another at the cut point.

7. The form edit unites two shots with two similarly framed objects that have similar shapes or movements. This is usually executed with a dissolve to show the audience how the objects look alike.

8. The concept edit unites two seemingly unrelated visual shots at a certain point in the story and the result is an idea, concept, or relationship in the mind of the viewer.

9. The combined edit is still just a cut, dissolve, or wipe at one transition, but it combines elements of several of the edit types. These make for rather powerful storytelling moments.

Chapter Four – Exercises & Projects

1. Acquire the media for a simple dialogue scene. Assemble it with straight cuts, fine tune the rhythm through trimming the tails and heads of the shots and watch your sequence. Now add dissolves at every cut point and watch the sequence again. How does it feel? Which way do you prefer and why?

2. Create any kind of wipe across an edit point for any two video clips in a sequence. Copy and paste those same two clips again in this mini-sequence and keep the same wipe effect. On the second instance of the wipe, add some sort of "swoosh" or other sound effect so the timings and duration feel

right. Watch both versions (without added SFX and with). Which do you prefer and why?

3. Record a variety of shots (LS, MS, MCU, CU) of a friend juggling, bouncing a ball or something that shows controlled and repeated subtle movements. Edit a brief sequence of these coverage shots with action edits, timing their continuity of action and movement as smoothly as possible. Practice using your trim tools at the cut points to really fine tune the illusion of uninterrupted action.

4. Take the action edit sequence from Exercise 3 and add one-second dissolves to each cut. Is the illusion of continuity maintained? If not, can you tweak the head and tail timings of the clips to smooth it out? What happens if you replace all of these dissolves with some kind of wipe effect? Does it change the continuity of action? Does it alter the pacing?

Chapter Four – Quiz Yourself

1. Name the four basic transitions discussed in this chapter.

2. What is a "jump cut?" What can cause it? When might you choose to use one?

3. What is the key component required of footage for you to create a "punch-in" / "cut-in" / "axial edit?"

4. What are head and tail "handles" and when might you need to access them?

5. In order to create a "form" or "graphic" edit, what kinds of images are required?

6. What kind of edit unites two matching shapes or compositions from two different shots across the transition?

7. What kind of edit places two unrelated images in sequence, but generates an "implied" meaning, thought, or feeling in the mind of the viewer?

Chapter Five
Editing Terms and Topics

Additional Editing Terms

- Sync Sound and Timecode
- Montage
- Parallel Editing
- Multi-camera Editing
- Composite Editing
- Rendering
- Chromakey
- Video Resolution

Additional Editing Topics

- Sound
- Color Correction
- Importing Still Images
- Digital Workflow
- Tools vs. Skills

These days, much is expected of an editor. Depending on the job size, budget, and purpose, many editors are tasked with performing more than just straight cuts. The increased sophistication and capabilities of the editing software have, in some ways, coerced the editor into expanding her/his skill set. Graphics creation, motion effects, music selection, and audio mixing may all be part of the modern editor's responsibilities.

Having covered many topics regarding shot type, shot quality, transition types, and edit categories, you are in a good place to go out and start editing. No one source of information will be able to tell you everything about the art, craft, and job requirements of an editor, but, by now, you should have a solid handle on most of the basics. In this chapter we will augment our list of topics by addressing some additional terms, concepts, and advice. Learning from a book is an excellent way to start wrapping your brain around the editing process, but there is no replacement for on-the-job training. The fun and satisfaction are to be found in the editing process itself, so get ready to go to work.

Additional Editing Terms

Sync Sound and Counting Time

Sync Sound

The term **sync** (short for synchronized or synchronous) has been used in filmmaking for a very long time. It usually refers to the synchronization between the picture track of the film and the sound track(s). If there is a mismatch in the sync, then the actor's mouth moves to say words but the words are not heard on the soundtrack at the same time. They are out of sync. Achieving and maintaining sync is a very important aspect of editing film and video.

Emulsion film motion pictures are shot with a camera that only captures the pictures on a strip of light-sensitive flexible plastic. A separate device is required to record the audio (now chiefly on digital recorders). This process is sometimes called "dual system" recording. These separate elements of picture and sound are eventually captured onto the computer and "married" together or "synched up" for the editing process. That is why we use the slate clapsticks to mark the "sync" point for the film image and the audio recording at the beginning of each take. Although video cameras have the capability of recording the picture and audio data onto the one tape or media file, many video-originated productions choose to record "dual system" as well – for quality control and for keeping camera and sound departments unencumbered by crossing responsibilities.

Once all of the "dual system" files are on the editing computer, the editor or assistant will have to sync them. There will be one frame of video that shows the clap sticks fully closed and there will be one "frame" of audio that has the sound of those sticks closing. The editor matches the picture "clap" frame with the audio "clap" frame and joins the clips together. From that point forward, the sync picture/sound clip can be edited together anywhere in the timeline. If no clap slate has been used, then the editor must search through the video clip for a unique "event" that shows something happening and then listen to the corresponding audio clip to hear that same something. This picture/sound "event" (like a clapping hand or a door slamming, etc.) will become the sync point for these media files.

Video cameras can record both picture and sound tracks to the one tape or digital media file at the same time. These elements are captured into your editing computer as separate media files that have references to one another and remain in sync for playback and editing. The software usually unites them by their timecode associations, but it is still your responsibility to keep them in sync while you edit. Depending on your software settings, trimming only one side of an edit with video track selected but not its corresponding audio tracks will cause this loss of sync. The mismatch becomes the exact number of frames that you remove or add to the video but do not also simultaneously remove or add to the audio. To fix a sync shift like this you could add or remove that exact number of frames to the audio tracks only at that cut point in your sequence. This exact number of out-of-sync frames is usually noted in the timeline of your editing software around the clips that have lost sync.

Counting Time

Emulsion film, being long strips of thin plastic, uses feet and frames (the unique space of a single image between perforations or sprocket holes) to count lengths and/or durations and therefore time. Videotape, having no perforations, uses a special track on the tape that counts time according to an electronic pulse that notes the hours, minutes, seconds, and frames (appearing as HR:MN:SC:FR, where the example of the one hour and 37 second mark on a tape would read as 01:00:37:00). Digital media files have similar "meta-data" embedded inside the file that keeps track of a great deal of information including the same time of hours, minutes, seconds, and frames, but does so digitally.

The frame rate for a particular format is also involved in this counting scheme. Emulsion film in the USA has a frame rate of 24 frames per second (24 fps) and the UK uses a rate of 25 fps. NTSC video in North America has a frame rate of roughly 30 fps (29.97) while European PAL video has a 25 fps rate. So for PAL projects on your editing software you would be able to watch 25 separate frames in one second and for NTSC projects you would be able to see 30. Of course, these frames would go by your eye so quickly in one second that you really do not get to distinguish one frame from another. You would have to step through one frame at a time to see the thirty individual frames of that second of video. Without getting too technical, matching frame rates are required for the syncing of emulsion film and its recorded audio (24 fps) and for video (PAL = 25 fps and NTSC is about 30 fps) and its optional, digitally recorded audio files. With the global adoption of HD (and whatever digital video technologies are on the horizon), you may see the likes of NTSC and PAL disappearing from the professional broadcast arena in the very near future.

Timecode (TC) is the counting scheme, or the clock, that video editing software uses to keep time for frame rate playback and for keeping sync. The picture information and the audio information (when they come from the same tape source or associated media files) will have the same matching timecode frame for frame. Depending on the recording camera and the medium (tape or hard drive), the timecode data may be set

Additional Editing Terms

to be unique per tape (hour one of shooting has 01 hour TC and hour two has 02 hour TC, or physical tape one has 01 hour TC and physical tape two has 02 hour TC, etc.), or each individual file may not have sequentially counting timecode but all are based on the same file-naming structure (i.e., all files start with 00:00:00:00 and count up to their individual durations, but have unique names and identifiers). Video editing software keeps track of all TC references and shows this data in the bins, in the playback windows, and in your sequence timeline. The project settings often dictate the counting scheme for your timecode on edited material and it is often best if they match frame rates, although newer software can mix frame rates in the timeline.

Montage

The term **montage** has several meanings when used in relation to motion picture editing. For the French, the word simply describes the act of assembling the film, which is the job of the editor. For many involved in Soviet silent cinema of the 1920s, it emerged as the Montage Theory of editing, which is a belief that two unrelated images can be edited together to generate a new thought, idea, or emotion in the mind of the viewer. An example of this concept edit was presented earlier in this book. A young couple announcing their wedding engagement in shot A is then followed by an image of a prisoner with a ball-and-chain around his ankle in shot B. A viewer might get the idea that the filmmakers are equating marriage with a prison term.

The more widely applied meaning of montage today refers to the **montage sequence**. This involves a series of quick clips, usually accompanied by music, that show a condensed version of actions over time. In a teen comedy it could be a series of shots showing the friends getting ready for the prom; in an action movie it could be a series of shots showing the elite fighting team going through tough training; in a romance it could be a series of shots showing a young couple going out on dates falling more and more in love with one another. A montage sequence serves a very useful purpose by condensing important plot points and developments that might otherwise unfold across a day, several weeks, or even years, into a shorter, more manageable duration. The audience does not have to watch every aspect of these events to understand their results. Think of it like a highlight reel of important plot events and building relationships that, if shown in their entirety, would take up way too much screen time.

Parallel Editing

Used primarily in fictional narrative filmmaking, **parallel editing** (also known as **cross cutting**) calls for a special construction where two plot lines of the story's action are inter-cut with one another. In other words, a portion of one plot line is shown, then the sequence shifts over to showing the other plot line which, in the film world, is supposed to be happening simultaneously. This technique proves especially effective during an action sequence – often a race against time. The pace of the sequence may also get more "frantic" as the two story lines unfold, building the suspense and getting closer to the dramatic climax. This can be achieved by making the shots in the sequence increasingly shorter and shorter. The frenetic energy of the cuts carries over to the audience member who is feeling the urgency of this pacing and the race against time.

Multi-camera Editing

Most fictional narrative filmmaking is accomplished with just one camera. The shot types described earlier in this book are composed, lit, and blocked for the one camera that is used to record the coverage for that scene. This can take a significant time to accomplish all of the shots needed to edit the scene for the movie. There is another practice, however, where multiple cameras are used on set to shoot different angles of the same action, getting differing shots of coverage while the actors perform the action one time on one take. Camera A records *Fred's* close-up and Camera B records *Sally's* close-up at the same time. Provided both performances are good, the production saves time and money shooting coverage in this manner. Using multiple cameras is very popular when recording studio-based situation comedies for television, soap operas, reality programming, news, talk shows, sporting and competition programming, live theatre, musical concerts and, with certain directors, on very "performance"-heavy scenes or stunt work in fictional narratives.

The beauty of multi-camera editing is that all of your source footage matches. A cut at any point will have a corresponding matching frame from another camera angle to cut to in perfect sync. Certainly all action should be seen from all coverage angles, but also the cameras may share identical **Timecode**, so at 00:24:17:00 (24 min. 17 sec.) a cut from one camera will have the next frame of image and time match for all cameras recording the event. Most professional video editing software has a built-in process for matching up all of your camera source footage. As a result, you have the option of cutting to any camera angle at any point in time, much the same as a television studio director in the control room has the option of switching from camera A to camera C to camera B, and so on. Because the audio was also recorded as one unbroken track during the performance, all of the camera images should match up perfectly while playing over the one source of audio.

Composite Editing

Think of composite editing as multi-layer editing where more than one image is seen on screen at one time. This will necessitate the use of more than one video track in your timeline and the use of visual effects or filters on the clips on the upper tracks. Your video project, or sequence, will have a set frame size based on the image resolution of the video format you are editing (see later in this chapter for more details). Most clips are going to have the same resolution or size and, if you stack one on top of the other, you will only see the top video track because it will block your view of anything underneath it. A visual effect/filter, such as a Superimposition or a Picture-In-Picture (PIP), will be needed to treat the upper track so that the lower track will at least be partially visible.

Split screen effects are created using this method. You could make two separate shots of people talking over the telephone fit into one screen by compositing the two clips on V1 and V2 of your timeline and applying some crop and reposition effects to each. A **PIP** inset is done in a similar fashion in which you reduce and reposition the video clip on V2 (see Figure 5.1).

Each video track in use counts as another data stream needing to be processed. The more compositing of video tracks you do in your sequence, the more difficulty the computer system will have playing back the multiple media files – this is especially true for high definition media. Most straightforward fictional narrative motion pictures will not need very much composite editing, but any projects that could benefit from multiple images or composited elements will need this approach. Music videos, sci-fi or fantasy, commercials, even corporate promotional and wedding videos may call on split screen, PIPs or composited visual effects (VFX). A **render** (see next section) may be required in order for the more complex stack of video clips to play back in sync on your system.

FIGURE 5.1 Composite edits are made out of multiple video layers like this example of a split-screen and the Picture-in-Picture over the background video track.

Rendering

Regardless of the video editing software that you use, some video or audio elements in the timeline will eventually need to be rendered during an edit session. Rendering is the creation of new media files that will allow the system to play back complex effects or composites more easily. Typically, if you have created a complicated visual effects composite of six HD media streams (V1 up to V6) the system may have difficulty playing it in **realtime**. The software is trying to heavily manipulate each pixel of each frame of each layer in the composite all at the same time. If you render the affected clips the system creates a brand new single "merged" media file that shows the result of all effects in the composite.

These rendered files do fill up space on your media drives, so be aware of that. Also, if you make a change to any content in a rendered clip or effect composite it "unrenders" or reverts back to the original complex media file references. Render times vary depending on the power of your system, the complexity of manipulation by the effects, and the complexity of the original source media. Don't be surprised if it takes a while.

Chromakey

When you watch a meteorologist deliver the weather report in front of a large radar image showing swirling patterns of cloud movement, you are seeing the result of a **chromakey**. You may be more familiar with the terms green screen or blue screen. These names refer to the same process where a certain color (chroma) is "keyed out" or removed from a video image. Post-production software is used to select that particular color (most often green or blue) and turn it invisible while the remaining pixel data in the image is untouched. This layer of "keyed" video becomes the foreground element (the weather person clip on V2) or top layer in a composite. Then, some other video image (clouds on radar clip on V1) is placed on the layer below to become the visible background of the new composited video image.

Although you could "key" any color in your video clips, the colors green and blue are most often used because they are two colors whose range of hues are not normally present in the skin or hair of human beings. Be advised that people with green or blue eyes will have their irises disappear if a similar green or blue color of chroma-screen was used during production. Another type of key, known as a Luma-Key, uses a low black video voltage (sometimes called "super black") to make this transparency. You may find this used on graphic elements where the super black pixels can be turned invisible by your editing software while "normal" video black pixels remain unaffected.

One could also create these still graphics with Alpha Channel instead of creating "super black" Luma-Keys.

Video Resolution

A video image is made up out of a grid of tiny boxes each filled with particular contrast and color data. These tiny boxes are called **pixels**, which is shorthand for picture elements. The more pixels of data you have in your image, the higher the resolution it will have. A high resolution means a greater ability to show more precise detail. High Definition (HD) video, in today's technology market, is a moderately high resolution capture and playback format for digital motion imaging on television and the web.

Video resolution is customarily represented by two numbers, the number of pixel units arranged horizontally across the screen's grid by the number of vertical lines (or rows of pixels down the screen). Full HDTV is represented by the resolution 1920 x 1080. This means there are 1,920 tiny pixel boxes arranged horizontally from the far left of the image to the far right of the image in a single row. Then there are 1,080 rows stacked up from the bottom of the frame to the top. Simple math tells us that a total of 2,073,600 pixels are used to make up the entire image. In comparison, Standard Definition digital video has an image resolution of 720 x 480 (North American NTSC-DV) and 720 x 576 (European PAL-DV), with an overall pixel count that is just a small fraction of that for HDTV. As a quick technical note, SD video uses rectangular, or nonsquare, pixels, while HD, graphics editing software and computer monitors use square pixels for creation and display of images.

More pixels may mean more detail, but it also means more data per frame to be analyzed, processed, and displayed by your video editing computer system. Even a robust system can handle only so much information in the processing pipeline (hard drives, processor, RAM, graphics card), so editing with full resolution video can slow things down. Most editing software allows you the option to convert your original files to a more compressed version. The pixel count will remain the same, but the amount of data represented in each pixel is filtered/averaged down so the system does not have to think as hard. For playback as streaming web videos the compression may also involve converting to a lesser frame resolution, so the final video media file has a smaller overall size in megabytes. An accompanying loss of visual quality may also be detected in the smaller video file.

Additional Editing Topics

Sound

Sound in motion picture creation is extremely important. Entire books are written on the subject of sound editing in movies and television, and awards are presented to people who do it well. The following topics should provide you with a basis for an approach to sound editing.

Earlier, in Chapter Three, we discussed the tea kettle whistle as a motivator for the edit. Beyond being a source for motivation, the sound track is a powerful component within the storytelling architecture. It can help underscore the surface reality of the scene. Consider the following example: a woman is seen sitting in a noisy business office in a wide shot. There is a cut to her in an MCU. One would expect the noisy business office ambience to continue to be heard under the new MCU of the woman. If the audience is not presented with that continuity of audio, they could be pulled out of the viewing experience, wondering what happened to the sounds. The cut would draw attention to itself in a negative way.

What if the same scenario occurs except this time there is no office noise after the cut, only dreamy, ethereal music is heard? This new audio information seems to match the calm look on the woman's face. This peaceful music is her internal sound track – it is representational. The audience is given new information about the internal mental or emotional state of this woman. Somehow, within all of the office craziness, she is staying calm and collected in a meditative state. The editor has used sound to draw positive attention to the transition through providing the audience, and the woman, with a break from the office noises (see Figure 5.2).

FIGURE 5.2   The noisy office sounds drop away at the cut giving way to mystical music to reflect the woman's inner peace.

So sounds can make statements that go against the visuals being presented to the viewer. Consider this example: you have an interior medium 2-shot of a man telling his friend that he is "going to hunt for a job." The ROAR of a lion is heard on the sound track and a picture transition takes us to a wide shot of a crowded, bustling city street during commuter rush hour. Animal noises are mixed in the sound track with the busy street ambience. The character from the previous shot, the job hunter, is now out in the wild on the hunt for a new job. If detected, an audience might normally wonder about the animal sounds playing while watching a busy city street, but because it follows the context of the job hunt, the out-of-context animal sounds actually become story-enhancing sounds (see Figure 5.3). They underscore the metaphorical big city "jungle" theme being explored in the story.

As with our train whistle example in Chapter Three, the lion's roar from the sound metaphor above presents another sound bridge. The roar takes us from one shot into another. In these examples, the sound of the next shot is heard before the picture of the next shot. We call this sound leading picture. The opposite holds true as well. You may have the sound of Shot 1 carry under the newly visible picture of Shot 2. We call this picture leading sound. Perhaps you have a wide shot of a man dropping a bowling ball on his foot. As he yelps in surprise, you cut to an extreme long shot of treetops in

FIGURE 5.3 The lion's roar bridges Shot 1 to Shot 2, which continues the animal sound metaphor. What it might look like in your sequence timeline.

FIGURE 5.4   The yelp of the man bridges across the edit and laps under the split picture track.

the forest. As the sound of his yelp continues under the new picture of treetops, flocks of birds fly up and away as if startled into flight by the man's cry carried so far across the countryside (see Figure 5.4).

The editing practice of having either picture or sound start early or end late is known as creating a **split edit**, an **L-cut**, or **lapping**. Picture and sound tracks are really separate media streams when they live inside your editing software. In most scenarios they will play in sync and be placed in the timeline together. It is easy to see how you then might end and begin both picture and sound track(s) for two shots at the same moment in time. This is called a **butt-cut** or a **straight cut**. Assemble edits and maybe the rough cuts will most likely be all butt-cuts. As soon as you start to finesse the timing of shots in the fine cut you may find that offsetting the cut point for the picture or the sound is advantageous, or sometimes necessary, especially during dialogue editing. You are making split edits for creative purposes. One track leads or follows the other. When done correctly, these can make your transitions either very engaging or very smooth for the audience. When done incorrectly, they can put the brakes on pretty quickly (see Figure 5.5).

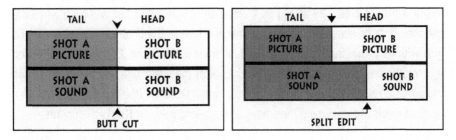

FIGURE 5.5   An example of the butt-cut becoming a split-edit.

Additional Editing Topics

Color Correction

A key component to the Finishing phase of post-production, Color Correction allows for an editor (or a special technician known as a Colorist) to tweak the contrast and color of the final clips in the video sequence. The term "correction" is usually applied to making major changes in the color of an image (removing too much blue near the windows on an interior shoot or too much green on a person's face in a grassy exterior shoot). The term color "grading" (or "timing") is also used during this phase, and refers to making creative alterations in the contrast and color values so a special "look" can be achieved (dark and moody; desaturated color palette; bright and super-saturated, cartoon-like colors, etc.).

Whether it is correction or grading, the main goal of this process is to get the video to have the desired look. This is motivated by both technical and aesthetic reasons. It is much more complicated than this, but video cameras basically capture and record light information as electronic voltages based on the quantity of light energy obtained from the different wavelengths of the visible spectrum. If the film set is dark then there isn't much energy (voltage or signal) present to record the scene and it may appear dark with weak color data. If the film set is very, very bright (a lot of energy and therefore voltage) the video image may appear too bright and washed out. As an editor, you would most often hope that the production team recorded images that represent the full spectrum of shadows, mid-tones, and highlights, and had adequate color saturation. When you have an appropriate amount of energy to manipulate, the color correction tools in your video editing software can do more with the signal and yield the desired look of the project.

There are two main parts to the video signal: Luminance and Chrominance. The luminance refers to the light levels or contrast and brightness of an image. Gauged along the gray scale, an image with good contrast should have areas that are representative of black shadows, mid-tones of gray, and bright, white highlights. A high contrast image will have both very strong dark areas and bright areas but will have very little mid-tone gray present. A low contrast image will have the reverse – mostly mid-tone gray with very little truly black or truly white areas in the frame. During color correction it is traditional to first establish the black level of the video signal (the "set-up"), then the white level (the "gain"), and thirdly the gray mid-tones (the "gamma"). With your contrast levels set you would then move on to making color (or **Hue**) adjustments.

Keeping it simple, chrominance, or color values, are manipulated by different tools in the software. They allow you control over actual color or hue values from the color spectrum. They also allow you control over voltage of a color, or its saturation level.

Desaturating a video image (removing all color voltages) turns it black and white. Saturating an image (driving up the voltages or boosting the color signals) amplifies the color content and can make them look unnaturally "thick" or "deep" like a candy apple red. The voltages, for both luminance and chrominance values, should not be over-driven or under-driven or they can compromise the quality of the video playback on electronic displays such as television and computer screens. There are devices called video scopes that help you measure and analyze the video signal and help you keep it within the "legal" zone.

Color correction provides you the opportunity to make bad video look better and to creatively "paint" a contrast and color 'look' for your overall video project. You can work your way through your sequence doing shot for shot and scene for scene correction and grading. The flesh tones of your subjects should look right, the color palette should look as you wish, and the shadows and bright areas should be where you want them. If your edited program is going to ever air on television, then you would absolutely want to color correct your sequence, but any video project, even just for web distribution, can benefit from the tweaks of the color correction phase of post-production.

Importing Still Images

Common still photographic digital cameras are capable of recording very high resolution still imagery. As an example you may have a still photographic digital file that is approximately 3500 x 2300 pixels. Even if you are editing in a full HD 1920 x 1080 video project, the video resolution (and frame size) is much smaller than the still photo you want to add to your sequence. What if you have downloaded an image file (like a .GIF) from a web site and you intend to add that file to your timeline? The web image is only 200 x 200 pixels – far smaller than the HD video frame. Each video editing application handles the import and still photo conversion process differently.

As a video editor you may be asked to add such still photographic images to your project. You may use a photo editing application to make cropped copies of the original photos so they take on the pixel dimension and frame size of your video project (i.e., a 1920 x 1080 cropped photo will import and fit into your HD video sequence). Depending on your video editing software, the imported file may come in to your project as a reference to your full resolution original photo and you can use a filter/effect to scale and reposition the larger photo so it fits into your video frame area. Other applications can be set to import converted versions of the original file and force it to resize to fit within the video frame, either on the horizontal or vertical axis, depending on the dimensions of the original photo file. Very small photos (like 200 x 200) will not scale well (expanding pixel data degrades image quality) and if you need to incorporate them you should know that they will remain very small even in an SD video project.

Additionally, a still photo is only one frame, but it does not play as only one frame in the video sequence. That would be a meager blip of 1/30 of a second or so. The import process may create new media of a longer duration where that one still frame is replicated to play over and over and over again as multiple instances of the same frame. So, if you need three seconds of that imported still image in your sequence you can edit a clip segment of three seconds into your sequence.

Digital Workflow

The power, flexibility, and relative convenience that editing software has brought to the world of visual media creation are undeniable. It is not all fun and games, however. There is a responsibility, often placed upon the editor's shoulders, to be organized and knowledgeable about file types, media assets, and interoperability of various software applications. This creation, storage, and sharing of video and audio materials is generally referred to as **workflow**. It is increasingly rare for post-production workflows to incorporate **analog** source materials (like physical strips of motion picture film prints or analog video tape). Most independent software users and post-production facilities are now deep into the digital workflow, where all video and audio elements needed for a story are created, stored, used, and authored as digital files on computers.

Today's multiplicity of digital video cameras uses many different encoders and file types to create their amazing high-resolution imagery. Not every version of digital video editing software uses the same types of files and not everyone encodes, stores, or accesses these files in the same way. A modern editor, in addition to being a great storyteller, must also be knowledgeable about these file types, feel comfortable with general computer operations, and understand media drives, cloud networking, and so forth.

The user-assigned details can also make a huge difference in how smooth the workflow becomes. Naming conventions differ from place to place, but logic dictates that developing a sensible and concise method for naming projects, bins, sequences, clips, folders, graphics, source tapes, etc., is essential. With clarity in your names and organization of your raw, digital materials, you are already well on your way to a more comfortable digital workflow for the life of your editing project.

Technology vs. Creativity

Film editing has been around for over one hundred years and videotape editing for about fifty. Computer-aided or digital non-linear editing has its origins around 1990. The one thing all of these techniques/tools have in common is that they are all a means of assembling a story of some kind to be shown to an audience. The editors, over the years, have been the skilled craftspeople, technicians, and storytellers using these devices and techniques – to show a story. The tools they have used have simply been a means to an end.

Today, in the digital age, the tools are different, but the skills of the persons who use them remain the same, or at least they should. Unfortunately, many people get lost in the nuances of the latest editing software and they separate the importance of their storytelling abilities from their knowledge of the computer's functionality. Or worse, they get so caught up in learning the latest bell or whistle in a specific editing application that they forget their primary goal as a storyteller. No one should confuse button-clicking abilities with solid editing skills.

There is a wide variety of video editing software available on the market today. Several are of professional grade quality and are used by high-end, post-production facilities, television networks, movie studios, and the like. Many are geared for more in-home/consumer use and have fewer capabilities. Knowing how to use several of these applications will benefit the newbie editor. Knowing one is a great start, but knowing more about using several editing applications from the high end is going to expand your job prospects considerably. The important thing to remember is that no matter what tool you end up using to perform the actual edit, at that point in the filmmaking process, you are in control and you are the creative force behind the story.

Additional Editing Topics

Chapter Five – Review

1. Timecode from original sources allows you to maintain sync between your picture and sound tracks within your edited sequence.

2. A montage sequence is a series of quick clips, usually accompanied by music, that show a condensed version of story-related actions and events that would normally happen over a longer period of "story" time.

3. Parallel editing cuts two, simultaneous story plot lines together so that concurrent action can be seen by the viewer at one time during the program. Usually done for action sequences.

4. Multi-camera editing allows you to edit footage of the same event captured all at the same time by several cameras. Useful for sports events, rock concerts, soap operas, dance sequences and staged situation comedy television programs.

5. Composite editing refers to creating a stack of video sources in a sequence where the application of filters/effects allow you to see portions of all of the clips at once in one frame.

6. Depending on your video editing software and hardware performance, you may need to render more complex HD video clips or composited VFX segments in your timeline. The software generates new, easier to play, media files.

7. Chromakey effects remove a particular color value or shades of a hue (most often green or blue) from a video image and allow the transparency of that color region to show video elements on the lower video tracks of the timeline.

8. All video formats have a screen dimension referenced by its width in pixel units by its height in lines or rows of pixels. For instance, HDTV has 1920 x 1080 video resolution.

9. Basic controllable properties of sound in video editing software are volume levels and panning (left and right channels).

10. Split-edits or L-cuts change the "start" time of the picture track or sync sound tracks for a clip in the timeline. If picture leads sound, then the audience sees a cut to the next video clip while still listening to the audio from the previous clip. If sound leads picture (often referred to as a sound bridge), then the audience will hear the sounds of the next shot in the movie underneath the video they are still watching in the current clip.

11. Sound, whether matching the visual elements or contrary to them, is a great tool to enhance meaning in the story and to engage your audience on a different sensory level.

12. The color correction or color grading phase of post-production allows the editor to make all shots in the sequence look as they should for the needs of the program. Basic contrast and color balancing helps the images look better, both technically and aesthetically. Special color treatments or "looks" may be added (e.g., a cold environment can be given a steely blue/gray color treatment; a hot desert may be made to look extra "warm" orange-amber).

13. Digital still images may be imported into your video editing project, but be aware of the dimensions of the image vs. the dimensions of your video project's format. They may be smaller from the web, and they may be larger from digital still cameras, but few will exactly match the frame size of your video. Cropping, resizing and repositioning may all be required.

14. Become familiar and comfortable with the workflow needed for managing digital media assets and the creation of computer-based video edits. Thinking ahead and knowing your end result can save you some big headaches.

15. As an editor, do not let the complexity of video editing software get in the way of your good decision-making abilities and solid storytelling skills.

Chapter Five – Exercises & Projects

1. Create a Montage Sequence – Record video of a school or family event or simply the "happenings" in your town. Review the footage and pull your favorite clips. Assemble a montage sequence and add a piece of music appropriate to the mood and pacing of the visual elements.

2. Practice Parallel Editing – Create a scenario where a person is inside a location searching for something important and another person is outside, making their way to that location to pick up that very same important item. Cut the coverage of each individual as separate mini-sequences and get a feel for how they play back-to-back. Now create a new sequence using parallel editing (cross-cutting) techniques with straight cuts – nothing fancy. Watch this new sequence for pacing. Does it generate tension and suspense? If not, how could you tweak the shot selection and the timing of the shots to make it more suspenseful?

3. Use a duplicate version of your final cross-cut sequence from Exercise 2 and see where you can create effective split-edits or L-cuts on the audio tracks. Then color correct each clip in the sequence so it has good contrast and a neutral or balanced color spectrum.

Chapter Five – Quiz Yourself

1. What information is represented by the following timecode – 01:06:37:14 ?

2. Do you think a dissolve could be considered composite editing even though it may occur on a single video track? If so, why?

3. This may depend on your editing software, but can rendering an effect clip in your timeline generate new media on your media drive? If you change something about that rendered video clip will it "unrender?"

4. What are the two most common colors used for creating Chromakey transparencies?

5. What does it mean that Full HDTV is 1920 x 1080?

6. Should you first address the contrast (blacks, whites, grays) of a video image or the color values?

7. True or False? – Most digital still images you import will have the exact same frame dimensions as the video format in your editing project.

Chapter Six
Working Practices

The working practices presented here are commonly accepted guidelines, or good tips, for you to think about during the daily process of editing. Some offer specific techniques to follow, while others simply suggest some good habits you may consider as you work. You may not encounter these precise scenarios on every job, but you should be aware that they may come up. You will learn how to recognize them and you will find ways to deal with them appropriately. They have been developed over time and have been found to work within many editing styles and within different genres. Each edit should be viewed with fresh eyes and you will be left to judge whether or not these working practices apply to the project that you are editing.

It should be noted that in today's highly visual media marketplace there are many venues where motion images are displayed. The variety of television programming, webisodes, commercials, short films, feature films, documentaries, promotional videos, broadcast news packages, and so forth all require some degree of editing before they are experienced by the viewing public. As you advance in your editing career you will learn what each of these program types require for their individual editorial workflow and established styles, etc. Starting with the following section of working practices as a solid base, you will be in a good position to fine-tune and augment your own list of editing "dos" and "don'ts."

Finally, there will be cases where an editor has done everything right – the correct type of edit, the correct elements – so that in theory the cut or dissolve or wipe should work. But it does not. One of the skills of an editor is to analyze and find out why the awkward edit exists. Of course, it could be that an exact answer may not even exist, but it is still up to you to find a solution. Editing is not a perfect craft. There is always room for creativity and discovery, and that is part of the fun of the process.

1. Use shots with matching head room when cutting shot-reverse-shot in a dialogue scene.

Reasons

Let us assume that these clean single MCU subject shots are part of an established two-person dialogue scene. To cut from a shot with correctly framed head room to another shot with incorrectly framed head room will look as if one of the subjects has suddenly altered his or her height.

To cut from one take of character A with incorrectly framed head room to a good shot of character B and then back to another correct take of character A will make it look as if A is bobbing up and down (see Figure 6.1).

Solutions

The incorrectly framed head room shot is nearly impossible to correct. Video editing software may have the ability to resize and reframe the footage, but in this case, enlarging video frames can cause image quality to degrade. Perhaps some of the footage might be usable for cut-aways, if it is not too badly framed. If there is not more than one take of this action or dialogue delivery, the entire shot might have to be rejected and replaced by another, even if the speaker is not seen to be speaking. An over-the-shoulder two-shot (OTS–2S) may be a solution.

Exceptions

The exception here is when the two shots cut together both suffer from the same bad head room framing. Obviously, if the head room is completely wrong, the shots may not look traditionally well-framed, but because the editor may not be able to do much about it, throw caution to the wind and go for the shots with the best performance regardless of head room. If the performance is engaging enough, most viewers may not even notice the differences in framing.

FIGURE 6.1   Beware of head room issues when cutting 'answering' coverage shots of a dialogue scene.

2. Avoid shots where distracting objects appear to be too close to the subject's head.

Reasons

This is a question of shot composition that has failed at the shooting stage. As an editor, you will not be able to change this questionably composed image. The presence of unwanted lines, shapes, objects, signs, etc. in the shot's background can be rather confusing or distracting to the viewer. It may also result in a humorous reaction not wanted by the filmmakers at that time. If offered such a shot, it is best not to use it if at all possible (see Figure 6.2).

Solutions

There really is no solution to this problem short of using some special effects like a Picture-In-Picture, split-screen or some kind of masking and blur that crops or obscures the offending background object. Of course, if the filmmakers made such a composition intentionally, then it would be appropriate for use.

Exceptions

You may be able to use this shot if it has a very shallow depth of field and the background (containing the offending object) is almost completely out of focus. The only other possible use is in a fast montage, where the shot is seen only for a very brief period of time.

FIGURE 6.2   Poor shot composition is not the fault of the editor, but the choice to use any of these shots in the final edit does fall under her or his domain. Omit, effect, or just go for it, but be aware of the possible consequences.

3. Avoid shots where the side edges of the frame cut off the heads or bodies of people.

Reasons

This type of framing may be considered aesthetically unpleasing by many who would watch, but that would not be your fault for you did not shoot the footage. Attempting to use closer shots (medium shots, medium close-up) that have such framing will cause complications for the edit. When the partial face of a character is in one shot and then that same face needs to be cut to for the next shot, it will cause a jump cut or potentially a continuity problem with action, line delivery, performance, or screen direction (see Figure 6.3).

Solutions

Sometimes the shot can be used, but it depends what comes before and what comes after. It also depends on the duration of the shot and the type of motion media project being edited.

Exceptions

These shots could be used in music videos, commercials, experimental films, and maybe in quick-cut action scenes, or where clips before and after do not cause a jump cut.

FIGURE 6.3 Compositions like these can make a smooth edit tricky. Try to avoid using footage that contains missing heads or where portions of faces are only partially visible.

4. Cut matched shots rather than unmatched shots in a back-and-forth dialogue scene.

Reasons

As you edit coverage from a traditional dialogue scene between two characters, you will most likely move in from a wide two-shot to tighter singles or over-the-shoulder shots. This allows the audience to get more familiar with the characters and their actions/reactions during the scene.

Established film grammar would suggest that the production team shot matching coverage of each character for this scene (this is not always the case, but let us assume that we have these within the footage you are editing). It is possible that you may have been given a variety of shot types for each character (medium shot, medium close-up, close-up, over-the-shoulder, etc.). Matching shots, when recorded with similar focal lengths, at similar distances from the subject, and under similar lighting conditions, often yield similar frame composition, focus depths, and so forth. An audience likes to see two similar shots cut together as opposed to two mismatched shots within the same scene's back-and-forth dialogue. It creates a coherency and a flow to the visual imagery.

In overhead diagram 1 of Figure 6.4, two people are standing having a conversation. Camera positions from placement 1 and placement 2 are at a similar distance from each subject – character A and character B. Both the shots are taken, for example, at a narrow lens angle (telephoto or long focal length) and both the shots are framed as a medium close-up. When this is the case, the editor will have subjects roughly the same size in the frame and backgrounds that are both out of focus to the same extent. The audience gets to place its attention solely on the speaking characters.

In overhead diagram 2, the camera position for placement 2 has changed. The shot composition should remain the same – a medium close-up. So at the new camera set-up 2, the lens angle will now have to be wider (shorter focal length). In this case the background may be in focus and the perspective on the distant background may be altered. Consequently, the editor would be cutting from a medium close-up with an "out of focus" background to a medium close-up with an "in focus" background.

Additionally, the perspective on each character plus the included field of view of background elements will not match.

Solutions

If a selection of good shots is available, then preference should be given to those with similarity in the quality of framing, focus, lighting, and perspective. If not, then see if you could cut-away or insert some other shot in between to "distract" the audience from noticing the dissimilar shots.

Exceptions

The exception to the practice is where a wide angle must be used to show a subject movement from foreground to background or the other way around. Generally, with significant available light, the wider the lens angle used, the more the picture background is in focus. In other words, the depth of field is greater (see diagrams A in Figure 6.4).

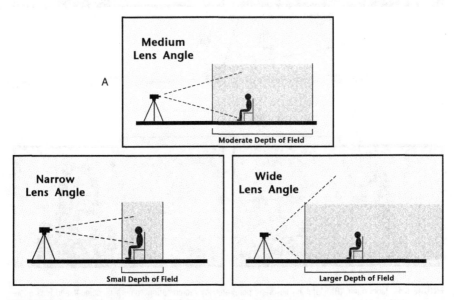

FIGURE 6.4   (Diagrams A) The depth of field changes with focal length.

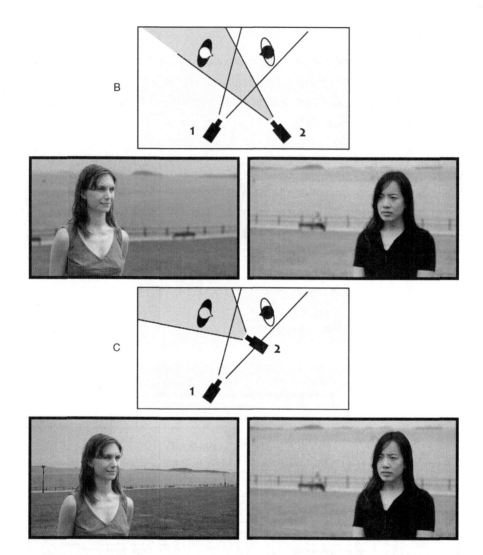

FIGURE 6.4 (continued) (B) Matching coverage generated by reciprocating camera placement and lens angle of view. (C) Mismatching coverage due to altered camera distance and focal length.

5. When editing dialogue, avoid automatically removing a performer's pauses.

Reasons

There are some things that can disrupt a performance, and this is one of them. The performer will have rehearsed the script to achieve a certain emotional state in the scene. Actors rightly claim that the space between words is just as important as the words themselves. Most of the time, the pauses are used to create weight, significance, or to add drama to the words or the scene in general. To automatically edit out these spaces (or beats or pauses) in a monologue or dialogue can completely change the intended meaning of the scene.

Solutions

Accept the pauses as a guide for your edits and, perhaps, use them as a motivation to incorporate a cut-away. Seeing some other subject, as in a reaction shot or "noddy," will maintain visual interest while keeping true to the pace of the actor's spoken performance. Accept the pauses as an important integrated element in the dialogue and not just as a moment when someone is not speaking.

Exceptions

The exceptions may have to do with the lack of time. In non-fiction programming like news, documentary, short-form commercial, and current affairs programs, where the maximum amount of visual and verbal information must fit into the minimum amount of time, the editor may choose to edit out unnecessary pauses.

It is very important to note that an editor may also remove, add, shorten, or lengthen "pauses" for the purposes of reconstructing the scene with a new rhythm and pacing of line delivery. Although the subject's performance is highly valued, the editor has the responsibility of sculpting the best story and character representations in the scene and across the entire motion picture. Playing with time, word order, and word placement can be beneficial.

6. A reaction shot seems more natural during a phrase or sentence than at the end.

Reasons

Each consecutive shot should convey some new information to the viewing audience. During a dialogue scene, just because one person is speaking does not mean that they are always providing new visual information. To help keep the audience engaged, it can be useful to cut to something new, such as the reaction shot of the other character listening. Breaking up a long line delivery with the reaction shots of the other character(s) involved in the scene can provide a certain rhythm and show new information about the state of other characters in the scene.

If you show only one person speaking, then cut to the other person's reaction over silence, then cut back to the first person who starts speaking again, and so on and so on, it will become rather monotonous for the viewer – too much straight back and forth like a tennis match.

Solutions

Look at and listen very carefully to the footage to find a motivation, however small, to insert a cut-away of the listener reacting. The reaction shot of character B is visible over the continuing dialogue of character A. If the cut-away is close to the end of the speaker's words, then this clip may become the next shot where the character B may actually be seen to speak as well. This type of dialogue editing with lapping picture and character line delivery is more interesting to the audience because it shows communication between the subjects, with both actions and reactions.

Exceptions

There are times when a single character does the majority of the speaking in a scene. If the performance is powerful enough to "carry" the scene, then by all means leave the line delivery uncut for the stronger emotional effect on the listening audience. Also, there may be a monologue delivered by one individual. If that performance is powerful enough, let it ride.

7. Do not be too bound by dialogue when looking for a cut point.

Reasons

In dialogue footage, there are two major motivations for cutting – vision and sounds. During a two-person dialogue, actions and reactions will take place. If you only cut when one character's words are finished, then it can become predictable or boring. While one person is talking, the other will be listening and may show facial reactions, provided that the production team shot such footage. These reactions are very important and can be used as the motivation for the "back and forth" editing for the scene.

Solutions

In fictional narrative shooting, it is common to record the close shots of one character's dialogue delivery with an off-screen performance of the lines for the unseen character. The audio for the off-screen character will not be used, but the visuals of the on-camera talent will be useful. It will be during these non-speaking moments that an editor should be able to find the reaction shots for cut-aways in the scene. Also, it may be possible to lift some frames out of the beginning of the shot before "Action" was called, or from the end after "Cut," if the talent did not break character too early.

In documentary, news, and other "talking head" programming, if no facial reaction is evident during the question and answer period, then the director or producer will hopefully have shot what some people call a reaction **noddy** of the listener as safety coverage. Noddies are close shots of the listener simulating a reaction to what was said. A noddy may be movements of the head, eyebrows, etc. When noddies are cut into the dialogue with a motivation, they can look quite natural, but they do tip the scales of artifice in news editing.

Noddies are also useful to edit out parts of verbal information. For instance, they can be used to reduce the duration of an interviewee's answer or cover for the numerous "ums" and "ahs" that inevitably need to be edited out of the replies. There is no written rule about the duration of a noddy, so it more or less depends on the circumstances. Adding a cut-away shot that is too quick (maybe under two seconds) may seem jarring; too long, and the audience might wonder why they are not watching the speaker again.

Exceptions

An exception could be when the primary shot is a monologue. There will be no other character present in the scene to use as a cut-away. Also, for comic timing, a delay in the cut to other characters may build the tension/release dynamic of the "pregnant" pause.

8. In a three-person dialogue, beware of cutting from a two-shot to another two-shot.

Reasons

If offered coverage of a three-person dialogue scene which contains several two-shots, then in all likelihood the central character will appear to jump from one side of the screen to the other (see Figure 6.5). A shot taken from camera position 1 shows the center person (character B) on the right-hand side of the screen with character A on the left. If you now cut to another two-shot from position 2, then this shot will show the same character B on the left-hand side of the screen, with character C on the right-hand side. This is a screen placement jump cut for character B and can disrupt the visual flow of the shots and confuse or annoy the audience.

Solutions

Provided that other coverage shots are available, cut to a single shot of a person instead. For example, cut from a two-shot of characters A and B to a medium close-up of character C. Or, conversely, you may cut from a medium close-up of character A to a two-shot of characters B and C.

You could also cut back out to a wide shot of the entire trio in between both of the two-shots provided there is appropriate continuity.

Exceptions

There are no exceptions to this practice unless the style of editing for this project accepts and encourages such visual "jumps."

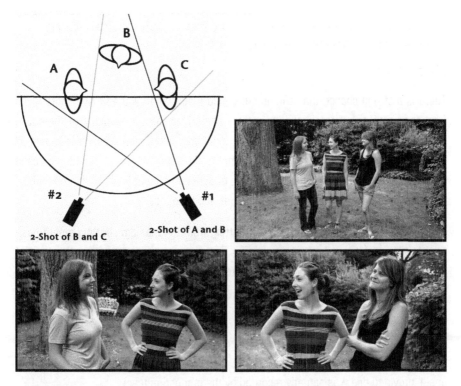

FIGURE 6.5 Three people covered by two two-shots will result in a compositional jump for character B from frame right to frame left at the cut point. Instead, use any other coverage to split the connection of the troublesome two-shots.

9. With a single subject, try to avoid cutting to the same camera angle.

Reasons

There is a strong chance that a jump cut would result when you edit two shots taken from the same or extremely similar camera angle (see the six elements of the cut in Chapter Three). This relates directly to the traditional film shooting practice known as the 30 degree rule, where each coverage shot of the same subject or object in a scene should come from the same side of the axis of action and be at least 30 degrees different in camera placement along the 180 degree shooting arc.

In example 1 of Figure 6.6, for example, cutting from the medium shot at camera position A into a medium close-up at position B could present a problem in the form of a jump cut. Cutting from a medium close-up to the medium shot, however, is less of a problem.

Solutions

It would be better to cut to a shot of the medium close-up from a different camera angle, provided one was actually recorded by the production team.

In diagram 2 of Figure 6.6, camera placement B has moved to the right, creating an angle on the talent that is more three-quarter frontal. If a shot from this position were available, the cut to the new angle would be more traditional and the risk of a jump cut reduced.

In the case where an alternate angle shot does not exist, then a cut-away could be used to separate the medium shot and the medium close-up of the same character on the same lens axis. This cut-away (of something appropriate to the scene) will allow the audience a visual break and the jump cut effect will not be experienced. This practice is more or less acceptable if you cut in to the medium shot from the medium close-up.

Exceptions

One exception to this practice is when cutting two shots together that are *very* dissimilar, such as when a great distance is covered between the two shots set up along the same lens axis. Of course, for creative reasons, one could edit a series of cut-ins along the same lens axis to achieve a quick "punching-in" effect – a zoom without the zoom, as it were.

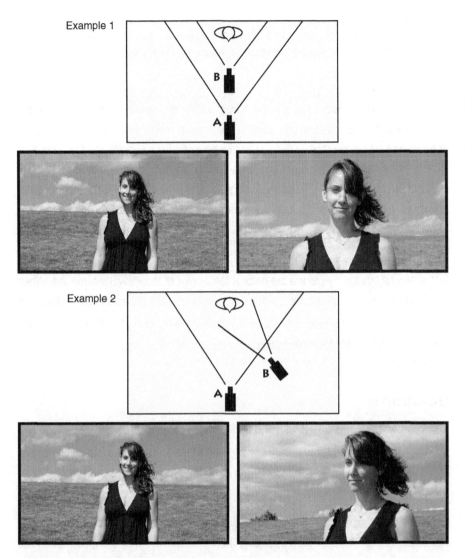

FIGURE 6.6 Example 1 shows a cut-in or an axial punch-in. Example 2 shows a more traditional shot option for the cut. A new angle and focal length help lessen the chance of a jump cut for the audience.

10. When cutting the "rise" as an action edit, cut before the subject's eyes leave frame.

Reasons

The "rise" is any movement of a subject from within the frame to up and out the top of frame and then across the edit point in continuous action. In these shots, the camera does not tilt up to properly follow the movements of the subject and the head gets cut off. For example, the subject sits on a park bench and then stands up, someone climbs the rungs of a ladder, a subject walks up steps. The action edit point could occur anywhere within the actor's total movement up until the eyes are about to break top of frame.

It would be advisable to keep the actor's eyes on screen for as long as possible in the first shot. The subject's eyes are the natural focal point of the viewer's attention. When they leave frame the audience loses that connection with the subject. Additionally, with no tilt up to maintain proper framing, the subject's head is cut off and this just looks odd to the viewer. This gets worse in close shots when the rise occurs very quickly due to the magnification of the head within the shot's framing.

Solutions

A woman is seated at a park bench. The edit point in shot 1 will be when her eyes approach the top of the screen, frame 1B, cutting to frame 2B in shot 2 (see Figure 6.7). This may seem only a short distance, but actually the subject leans forward before rising. This happens naturally.

If the subject's head is off the screen when the cut is made, frame 1C, then the edit will appear to be "late." If the editor cuts before movement, frame 1A, so that all the movement is seen on the medium long shot, frame 2A, then the edit may be deemed an "early cut."

In these examples, early cuts are not normally as disturbing as late cuts. Watching most of the action from the second (wider) shot is not so wrong, especially if the woman continues up and out of frame. However, the late cut example of shot 1C and shot 2C presents the issue of what the audience gets to look at during the last few moments of shot 1. Granted this transition will occur relatively quickly, but once the entire head clears the top of frame, the audience is seeking some new information. It wants to see the character's face again and watch the continuous action of the move.

Exceptions

One exception to this practice is when the first shot is closer than a medium close-up. It is rather difficult to cut smoothly away from a close-up or big close-up on a rise. An early cut is almost inevitable due to the size of the face within the frame and lack of physical space for the upward movement.

FIGURE 6.7 Examples of cutting on the rise.

11. When cutting to a close-up of an action, select a version of the close-up where the action is slower.

Reasons

If the action of the close-up happens at the same speed as that of the wider shot, then the speed of the action, as seen on the close-up, seems faster. This is due to the relative size of the object within the closer framing. It is now a large object so it has very little space to move within the close-up frame. Any quick or even "normal" movement would appear to happen too quickly because the object has less distance to travel around the screen before it breaks out through an edge. You are hoping that the production team understood this phenomenon and got some of the close-up takes at a slower speed of object movement.

For example, the subject is picking up a book in the wide shot (see Figure 6.8). The close-up shows the hand also picking up the book. The action on the long shot is at normal speed and the book never leaves the frame. But in the closer shot the book moves out of frame very quickly. So, if the close-up action is carried out at the same speed, it seems faster.

Solutions

You hope that the director has provided an additional close-up with a slightly slower action. The slower version will appear to move at a "normal" speed. If necessary, your video editing software may have motion effects built in that can slow down a shot just enough to be effective.

Exception

This practice does not apply to shots of moving machinery.

FIGURE 6.8 Be aware of speed of action in closer shots. Quick movement will not match the wider shots across an action edit. Shot 1 is a long shot of a woman picking up the book. Shot 2 is a close-up showing the woman with the book in hand.

12. Understand the visual differences between a tracking shot and a zoom.

Reasons

Many argue that a zooming image presents a very unnatural effect due to its uniform magnification of distant objects. It has no change in perspective, so that the horizon (or far distance) and the middle distance will come toward you at the same speed as any objects in the foreground. As our eyes do not zoom, the "movement" through film space can seem unnatural and stand out to a viewer.

A dolly tracking shot (sometimes called a truck in or a push in), on the other hand, is considered a natural movement that will have a perspective change and is analogous to what our normal vision would produce. The camera lens, like our eyes, is moved closer to the subject, who grows larger with proximity while the background remains "further away."

The two sequences of shots in Figure 6.9 show the difference between the zoom and the dolly tracking shot.

It is also a common practice for filmmakers to combine lens and camera support movement within a complex shot. A shot containing a zoom may also be used if it contains another camera movement at the same time which helps to camouflage the zoom.

Examples

- Tilt with a zoom
- Pan with a zoom
- Dolly crab with a zoom
- Pedestal or boom elevation with a zoom, etc.

Exceptions

An example of a non-traditional zoom is when it "creeps," i.e., when it is so slow that you actually do not realize it is a zoom. Slow zooms during long takes of slow action or dialogue-driven shots will evolve the composition over a longer time and the subtle changes in framing happen so gradually that a viewer will most likely not notice as they pay attention to the actors, etc. As an editor, you will find this type of shot relatively easy to cut in to the program in its entirety, or to cut up with other reaction shots as necessary, because the zoom will be so slow that cutting on the lens movement will most likely not be noticed.

A zoom in TV news or other "reality" type programming is another exception as it is more accepted within those genres. Obviously a detail of the content is the motivation to make the zoom.

In addition, a zoom used in a shot without any discernible background, e.g., a white wall or sky, might possibly go unnoticed.

ZOOM   DOLLY

FIGURE 6.9 Zoom movements will alter perspectives on the film space, especially the Background. Left column — zoom movement. Right column — dolly movement.

13. Beware of shots that track out without motivation.

Reasons

A dolly **track out** (**truck out**, or pull out) can often initiate a scene to show more of the location, or signal the end of a sequence or a scene. It may precede either a dissolve or a cut to another scene or even a fade to black. If no subject movement comes toward the camera initiating the track out (backwards), then the camera takes on a consciousness of its own. The audience may not be accustomed to the camera suddenly moving as if it were motivated by its own thoughts or desires (see Figure 6.10).

Solutions

The motivation for the track out will usually be included in the shot. In the case where no motivation is evident, or where motivation does not exist in the previous shot, see if the scene can live without that tracking shot.

Exceptions

If this is a visual treatment that has already been established in the motion picture (a free-moving camera with its own "motivations"), then it would be part of the style of the film and, therefore, appropriate to use. Another exception may be when a track out precedes a narrative jump in time, location, or tempo, or where the track out is the final shot of the production and is used partly as a background for superimposed end credits.

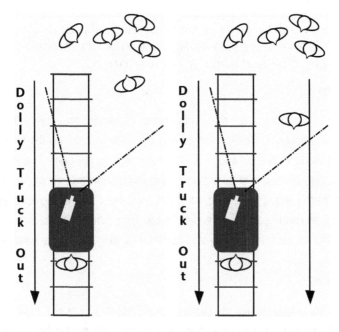

FIGURE 6.10   Understand how truck out dolly shots are motivated with subject movement and when they are not.

14. When editing in a pan or a dolly crab move, use the best version that is smooth, timed well, and leads the subject's movement.

Reasons

Dolly moves and panning shots that follow talent movement are often rather tricky to record during production. Several variables and different crew members, plus talent, are involved in their creation and it is easy for things to not quite flow as intended. When reviewing the takes of complex or developing shots like these, watch for the one with smooth camera movement, adequate lead room for the subject's movement, proper focus, and good pacing. An audience watching a bumpy move, a bad composition, or a blurry moment in the shot may have their viewing experience compromised.

Solutions

Again, an editor cannot change the quality of the shots that he or she is given, but must work with the material presented as best as possible. Seek out the best takes that are available that meet the criteria for such a shot. In some cases, you may use just the good portions of multiple takes and stitch them together with some cut-aways. If there are a number of takes, a shot should be selected where the camera has "led the subject" (see Figure 6.11), i.e., where there is more frame space before the subject than behind, has good focus throughout, and is smooth, with good pacing appropriate for the entire scene.

Exceptions

The exceptions to this practice may be found in fast-paced action shots, or even handheld cinéma vérité style shooting where the slightly "jerky" camera adds to a sense of immediacy, danger, or reality.

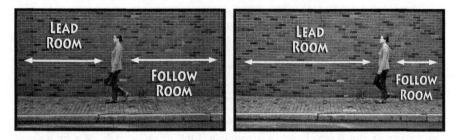

FIGURE 6.11   Select the crab dolly shots that provide stability, good focus, and ample lead room for talent movement.

15. Begin and end each pan, tilt, or dolly shot on a static frame.

Reasons

Cutting into a shot that is already in motion can cause a "jump cut" effect within the mind of the viewer. Cutting away from a shot that is in motion to a static shot can also be jarring, but it may be more acceptable if the narrative calls for such a visual treatment.

Solutions

The production team should provide footage of pan, tilt, and dolly shots that begin with a static frame, move for the duration of action, and then end on a static frame. This is not always the case, but as an editor you would hope for this scenario.

If shot 1 is a static, simple shot and you wish to cut to the complex moving shot (shot 2), then you should keep those static frames at the head of shot 2. This allows you to cut from static frames to static frames. The audience will treat this as an "invisible" edit because movement comes after the static transition.

At the end of complex shot 2, after the tilt, pan, or dolly move, you would most likely wish to finish that shot on the static frame as well. You may then cut to shot 3, the next static shot. This again provides an invisible edit for the audience – static to static.

Exceptions

If you decide to string several complex movement shots together, perhaps in an action sequence, then you will not be cutting static to static but moving to moving to keep the pace of the action going. One thing to watch out for in this scenario, however, is the speed of the camera movement and the subject movement within the shots you are cutting together. If the speeds are not matching or at least similar, this can cause visual interruptions to the flow of images and the audience may sense the shift in tempo.

FIGURE 6.12 The locked-off camera at the end of Shot 1 will help create an invisible cut into the static start frames in dolly Shot 2.

16. If a subject is moving within a pan, dolly crab, or truck, avoid cutting to a static shot of the same subject if they are then stationary.

Reasons

A cut from or into a camera movement may appear as a jump to the eye. A subject in motion in dynamic shot 1 but who is then shown as stationary in static shot 2 will appear to jump in time or space.

Solutions

Take, for example, a subject within a dolly move (Figure 6.13) who is moving in the direction of the crab. It is possible to cut to a static shot of the subject, but only when the subject has cleared the frame for a reasonable time prior to the cut. The end dolly of complex shot 1 should be static prior to the cut to the simple static medium shot 2.

There are two reasons for this. First, you may want to finish or clear the action in the shot before cutting out of the shot. Second, the pan or dolly is likely to be a complex shot. As such, like a developing shot, it should have a beginning (the initial static frame), a middle (the pan with another movement, tilt, or zoom), and an end (the final static frame).

The preferred place for the cut is on the static frame, where the camera is not moving even though the subject may be.

So, unless the camera stops, and/or the subject stops, and/or the subject is no longer in frame, then it is better if the next shot does not show the same subject as stationary.

Exceptions

There are many scenarios where this guideline may be overruled. Depending on the material involved, the program type, the pacing of the footage, and the pacing of the scene being cut, you may choose to experiment with cutting into and out of action and stationary shots. Most likely you will succeed in proving to yourself that it just does not look or feel right.

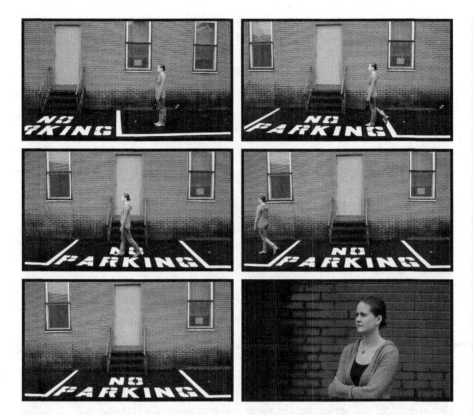

FIGURE 6.13 Allow the dolly action and subject movement to finish before cutting to a static shot of the same stationary subject.

17. Objects, like people, moving in a direction have an action line. Avoid crossing it or the screen direction will be reversed.

Reasons

Refer to the Screen Direction section in Chapter Two.

In diagram 1 of Figure 6.14, a conveyor belt moves boxes from frame left to frame right as seen from camera position A. The shot itself is shown in image 2.

If the line is crossed, i.e., taken from camera position B (see overhead diagram 1), then the belt appears to be moving the boxes from right to left (image 3).

Solutions

Select shots from one side of the line only, or use a neutral cut-away between the shots if the line must be crossed. A close-up of part of the machinery not showing the belt movement would be suitable. In documentary or reality programming you could also use a wipe to get from one side of the belt to the other.

Obviously, if the camera were to move from one side of the belt to the other during the shot, a jump cut will not appear, but the direction of the belt is still reversed.

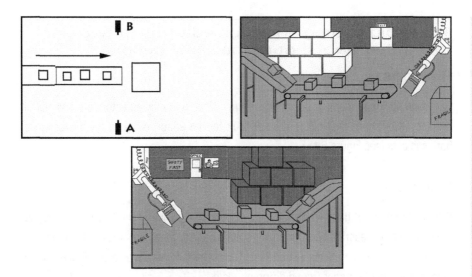

FIGURE 6.14 The machinery establishes a line of movement and a screen direction. Shooting from the opposite side of the initial 180-degree line would reverse the flow.

18. Avoid cutting an action edit from a two-shot to another two-shot of the same people.

Reasons

An action edit requires near perfect continuity. Once two moving actors are involved in the shot, it becomes that much more difficult for the editor to match the movement of both subjects (see Figure 6.15).

Solutions

When cutting out of the two-shot, cut to a closer shot of one of the two characters, cut to some form of reaction shot, or possibly cut to a very long shot if it exists among the footage. Trying to match the action for all concerned parties would be difficult if you went for another two-shot from a different angle.

Exceptions

A much wider shot of the entire environment, including the two subjects, is more likely to hide any incongruous body movements and so forth. Any event shot with multiple cameras may also alleviate this issue because action would match across a multi-camera edit. If the event where the action is occurring is frenetic enough (fight scene, war, fast dancing, etc.) then cutting from two-shot to two-shot may be perfectly acceptable with that sort of energy, confusion, or movement.

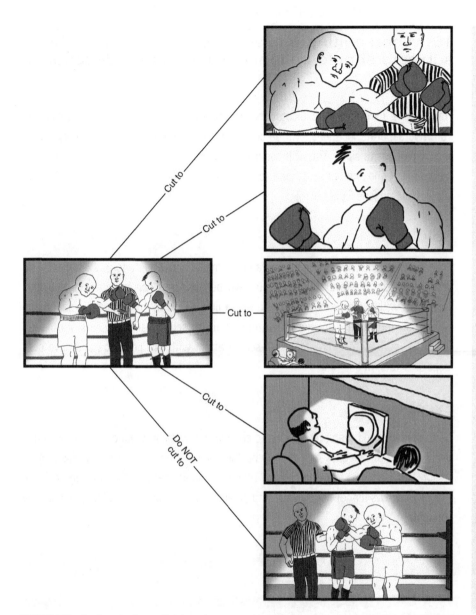

FIGURE 6.15 Cut from the first medium long shot to any other coverage shot but another medium long shot still showing all subjects.

19. When editing a telephone conversation, the subjects should be looking in different directions.

Reasons

Traditionally, film grammar indicates that the characters, speaking over the telephone from two separate locations, will be composed so they look across the empty frame, and from opposite sides. This will generate the idea in the viewer's mind that they are "addressing" one another across the screen as you cut from one single shot to the next and back again (see Figure 6.16).

Solutions

Hope that the composition of the footage for this scene was done in such a fashion. Otherwise, edit whatever material you have because you cannot alter the subject's placement within the frame unless you use a flop effect and reverse the video image horizontally (provided there are no written words on screen). If both shots are framed correctly, you may even create a split-screen effect with this coverage and have both faces on screen at one time.

Exceptions

There may be good dramatic reasons to change this working practice. If one person is shot with his or her back directly toward the camera, then the direction of the other person may be changed if the footage allows it. Additionally, if the coverage of each individual shows him or her moving around with mobile phones, then this practice may not apply.

FIGURE 6.16 Static telephone dialogue coverage of two persons in separate locations should be treated as if they occupied the same film space and were speaking to one another in person. Proper framing and look room should be present in the shots. Joining them together in a split screen can be easily achieved.

20. For any action edit, if a character exits frame left, then the same character should enter the next shot frame right.

Reasons

This is a very basic practice for any moving subject within the accepted film grammar. The continuity of screen direction, even across the transition, should be constant. It helps establish the directions of left and right within the film space and keeps the audience properly oriented within this fictional landscape (see Figure 6.17).

Solutions

The appropriate coverage with proper screen direction should be provided to you for the edit. If you do not get the shot with proper screen direction maintained, then you had better seek a diverting cut-away shot to place in between.

Exceptions

The exceptions to this practice are:

- The direction is actually seen to change on screen
- There is a suggested change of direction on screen followed by a cut-away
- The change of direction is caused by the cut-away (e.g., in the haunted house, running in one direction, seeing the ghost, then running the opposite way)

FIGURE 6.17   Screen direction should be maintained across action edits.

21. Beware of screen placement issues with an "object of interest."

Reasons

Even though the human subjects are on the correct sides of the screen in the coverage shots, the audience will have an additional visual reference, sometimes called the object of interest or the point of interest.

For example, a two-shot of a man and woman (shot 1) shows a painting that is framed center screen. Cutting to the man (shot 2) will show the painting screen left. Cutting now to the woman (shot 3), the object of interest (the painting) has jumped to screen right. Even though the edit is technically correct, the point of interest jumps, and this can be visually distracting.

Solutions

Where an object of interest is evident, either keep it in the same area of frame, or select the shots that either eliminate it altogether or minimize its onscreen presence (shot 4).

Exceptions

An exception to this working practice is where the object of interest is so small as to be negligible, where it is far in the background, or if it is out of focus. Another is where some other subject in the action of the scene covers the object of interest, either partially or totally.

FIGURE 6.18   Much like a person can "jump" sides of frame in a three-person "back-and-forth" dialogue, objects of interest can do the same thing. Try to keep to closer shots to hide the object jumping.

22. Edit in a wide shot as soon as possible after a series of close-up shots in a group scene.

Reasons

It can be easy for an audience to forget the exact location of subjects in the film space, especially during a fast-moving production. After a series of medium shots, medium close-ups, and close-up shots, particularly those with "out of focus" backgrounds, it becomes important to re-establish the scene's and the subjects' locations. If you choose to introduce a series of characters, all in close-up, then you would do well to show them all again grouped together in the wide shot.

Solutions

Be careful about editing an entire sequence with only close-ups — unless there is a need to do so.

Even one quick cut to a long shot, showing the relationship of the subjects to each other and to their surroundings, gives a much better grounding to the scene.

Exceptions

The exception to this practice is where the location or scene is well known to the audience, such as the main set of a popular TV show.

FIGURE 6.19   After a series of closer shots it may be helpful to show a wide shot to re-establish the scene in the viewer's mind.

23. Cut to a close shot of a new subject soon after they enter a scene.

Reasons

This may be the first time the character has been seen and the audience will not know the new subject. The audience needs to see this new entity with its new characteristics. This may be a person, a dog, a robot, etc.

A long shot will only show the character or subject in relationship to other subjects and to the location, but a new character needs to be shown closer to be identified.

Solutions

Edit in a closer shot of the character at the earliest opportunity. This also applies if the character is not new but has not been seen for some time. Support the audience by reminding them of events and people.

Exceptions

The obvious exceptions are when the character is an extra or a "bit" player, or needs to be kept secret for narrative purposes.

FIGURE 6.20   Inform the audience by showing them a closer shot of a new character entering a scene.

24. When editing a new scene with new backgrounds, show an establishing shot at the earliest opportunity.

Reasons

The audience not only likes to know what is happening in a new scene, but also where it is happening.

The audience benefits from seeing some form of visual "geography" that establishes the relationship between the environment and the subjects in the scene that unfolds there.

In short, some form of wide shot, for example, a long shot, a very long shot, or an extreme long shot, will be helpful. This wide shot should serve a number of purposes such as to give some geography of the scene, to show time of day or season of year, to establish the relationship of the character(s) to the surroundings, and/or to establish a general impression of movement of the subjects.

Exceptions

Obviously, if no exterior establishing shot was recorded then you will not have it to edit it in at the beginning of the new scene. You may also opt, for creative reasons, to not show an establishing shot but cut right in to the scene, perhaps in a close-up shot of some element within the set. Then you could pull back and show a wider shot of the location of the scene. This method creates more of an **anti-establishing** shot. It would stress audio ambience over exterior imagery while you are grounding the viewer in the new location, and makes for a refreshing change. If the scene is shown in closer shots and seems to take place in an unknown location, the actual establishing wide shot could be shown last as a sort of reveal and a surprise for the audience – perhaps for shock but more so for comic intent.

FIGURE 6.21 Using a wider shot to open a new sequence of scenes at a new location can help ground the audience and provide much needed information with one image.

25. Avoid making an action edit from a long shot of a subject to a close-up of the same subject.

Reasons

It is a jump cut to be avoided, unless a shock effect is required or unless the character is recognizable and identifiable in the long shot.

Example

In example 1 of Figure 6.22, the overhead schematic shows a man walking up to a car in a very long shot. He stops beside the car door to unlock it with his key. In two shots, it may look as it does in example 1 of Figure 6.22.

It will cut together, but it is too much of a jump to the eyes, and the visual reaction may be, "Who is this new man?" or "Where have the first man and the car gone?" Unless this character and vehicle are extremely well known to the viewing audience, this edit can break the visual flow and is therefore unacceptable.

It would be better to use three shots as shown in example 2: (1) the long shot to set the scene; (2) the medium long shot at a different angle to show more details; and (3) now that he is readily identified, back to the first angle and the close-up shot. The result of having the extra shot in between the two shots is to make the scene flow more smoothly. Now the audience knows who the man is, where the man is going and what he is doing.

Example 1

Wide shot from Camera A

Close-up shot also from Camera A

Example 2

Shot 1 – Wide shot from A

Shot 2 – Medium long shot from B

Shot 3 – Close-up from A

Example 1

Example 2

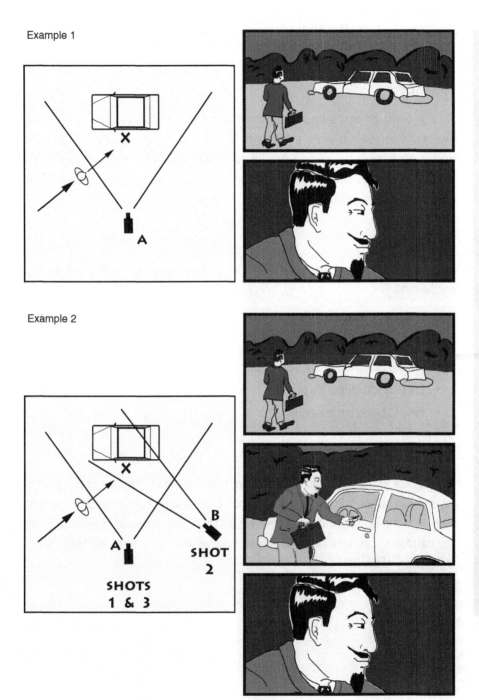

FIGURE 6.22 If the coverage has been provided, you may find it beneficial to cut three shots (long, medium, close) rather than just two (long, close) so the audience follows along with this series of action edits.

26. Beware of editing a cut to black followed with a cut to full picture.

Reasons

A cut to black is a very serious statement in narrative film production. Because it is an abrupt change over from visible picture to full black it carries with it a very dramatic weight, especially when you cut straight out of that black to a new, full image in the next shot. Reserve this bold treatment for an appropriate project whose visual style can absorb this dramatic editing practice.

Solutions

Some possible combinations for the end of a sequence or scene and the start of another are:

- Cut to next picture
- Dissolve to next picture
- Fade to black, fade up to picture (Dip to Color)
- Cut to black, fade up to picture
- Fade to black, cut to picture

Exceptions

The cut to black and cut to picture is used to break two entire programs, or two productions or two complete items from each other, or for a very dramatic effect. It is often used in editing feature film trailers because the shots that are joined together to advertise the movie were not meant to be joined together and cuts to black add to the drama and mystery of the story.

27. At the start of a program, the sound track can lead the visual track.

Reasons

Some claim that a picture without sound is dead, but sound without a picture is not. An audience, upon hearing the sounds (possibly music and ambience), will begin to imagine what is happening even before they know anything about it. The imagination is triggered. As the pictures then come on the screen, the multi-sensory experience begins.

Obviously this practice depends upon what the sound is and what the opening pictures are going to be in the program.

Exceptions

In short form (30 to 60 seconds) television advertisements, where the picture is obviously on screen as early as possible for time reasons. In general, television programming does not like to incorporate full black screens for too long because the viewing audience could mistake this for an actual technical error with the display device.

28. For the end of a program, use the end of the music.

Reasons

Music, of whatever nature, usually is divided up into different phrases, verses, or movements and will have a distinct structure. Part of this structure will be an ending or climax. This climax should be used to match the shots that end your video. It would be confusing to show the final pictures of a program with an opening musical passage that fades down. They would probably not match well.

Solutions

The music should be **back timed** to find its correct start point relative to the visuals of the sequence. If the timing is correct, the last bars of the musical piece should match the final shots of the sequence. This is especially true at the end of a program when the last bar of the music would be timed with the fade to black. Those more skilled in music editing may cut out the middle of a song and mix together the start and end to time best with the end of the motion picture.

Exceptions

The main exception to this practice is where the music is faded gradually into or under other sound, dialogue, or music that is stronger.

29. Put aside your edited sequence for a while and watch it again with fresh eyes.

Reasons

When you are an editor of a feature film or any long-form documentary piece, etc., you become "married" to the movie. You live with it day in and day out, sometimes for weeks or months at a time. You are often listening to the same sections over and over and over again. You grow to anticipate the words and the pictures until they no longer really stand out in your mind but are part of the editing "wallpaper." It becomes very easy to blind yourself to edits that are not working or entire sections that may play better in another location within the sequence.

Solutions

Time allowing, you would be wise to take a break from the editing process. A day or two away from the well-known material will help you forget the exact pacing, the cut points, the lines of dialogue, and so forth – perhaps not forget entirely, but you will be watching the piece with less anticipation. This respite should give you a pair of "fresh eyes and ears" to view and listen to your story. When you approach the same material with fresh senses, you may pick up on which edits are not working and which scenes within the piece may play better elsewhere.

Exceptions

Obviously, if you are involved with much shorter or more straightforward cutting jobs that have a "quick turnaround time," then you will not have the luxury of taking a day or two away from the material to refresh your senses. You will hope that an overnight break will be enough time away for you to be more critical of your own work come morning.

30. Use close-ups of subjects in a scene for the greatest emotional effect.

Reasons

The close-up of anyone's face is a very intimate shot. It carries with it a great deal of visual information and, depending on the expression of the face and the context within the story at that point, it can easily sway an audience emotionally. Using such a powerful shot too early in a scene's development could dilute the efficacy of those same shots when they are used later to make an emotional point or underscore a certain counter-current in the storyline through a reaction shot.

Solutions

Save the close-up shot of the character or characters for when an audience will benefit most from seeing the actors' faces in such intimate detail. The close-up will yield a clearer assessment of a character's emotional or mental state to the viewer. If the drama or tension of the scene is rising, cutting to closer shots toward the climax will provide the audience with more emotionally engaging visuals. This effect will be watered down if you go to the close-up shots too soon in a scene's development.

Exceptions

Documentary and news "talking head" interviews will be recorded mostly in medium shots and closer. You will have to use these shots right away in the sequence. Often, fictional narrative television and web programming will have significantly more coverage with close shots of individuals due to the smaller screen on which they get displayed. Cutting to such close-up shots sooner in each scene could be encouraged for television and internet programming. Additionally, if the lighting on a close-up of the character partially or entirely obscures the face for narrative purposes (to protect an identity, create mystery, etc.), then these shots should be edited in the sequence as required.

FIGURE 6.23   The Close-up conveys much emotional detail. Use where appropriate, but often later in the scene is preferable for greatest emotional affect on the audience.

31. Cut away from a subject soon after her "look" rests upon her object of interest.

Reasons

A shot depicting a subject looking at some object of interest off screen is the perfect set-up for a **reveal** to the audience. In general, you would cut to the shot of the object of interest next. The motivation for this edit rises out of the character's look and initial facial reaction to the yet-to-be-seen object off screen. Once the physical movement of head and eyes has come to a rest, the audience will likewise wish to see what is now being focused upon; hence the cut to the shot of the object (see Figure 6.24).

Solutions

The editor hopes that the actor was instructed during production to look off screen and react to some object. He or she further hopes that the talent achieves the look with a final solid head placement and **eye-line** to some object off screen. It is the solidity of the final look – the focusing of the eyes along a particular line – and a facial reaction of recognition that create the strongest cut point.

Exceptions

Clearly, if no take of the looking shot ends with a solid, strong gaze from the actor then you cannot cut away at the moment of the eyes' focus. You will have to find the most acceptable point of recognition on the actor's face and then cut. Faster action sequences or scenes that involve multiple objects off-screen would not necessarily call for a static head and focused eye-line from the actor.

FIGURE 6.24 Allowing the actor's eyes to lock on the off-screen object of interest generates a need within the viewer to also see this new object. This motivated cut to the object of interest is often called a reveal.

32. In documentary programming, edit out "ums" and "ahs" in interviewee speech.

Reasons

Often your goal as an editor, especially in documentary programming of real people, is to make them look and sound as good as possible on screen. A fourth grader, a diplomat, or a scientist may all have certain verbal pauses in their vocalized speech patterns. They may say "umm" or "ahh" to fill the space between their thoughts. While listening in person, these verbalized pauses often go unnoticed unless they are extremely excessive. Watching a short answer filled with "umm" and "ahh" will be more noticeable and less appealing to the viewer, and it can waste valuable time to get to the point.

Solutions

Edit out these verbal pauses in documentary or non-fiction material whenever possible. If the mouth does not move very much while the sound is made, lift the "um" "ah" or "gulp" and let the **room tone** or ambience track mask the hole. If the offense is more visually noticeable, then you may have to cut away to a graphic or some **B-roll**, or to an interviewer "noddy" shot if such a thing exists. The B-roll cut-away is a staple of documentary monologue editing so that the verbal points of the person speaking sound clear, concise, and coherent.

Exceptions

Occasionally, someone's speech pattern and the verbal "tics" they may exhibit are inextricably tied to their persona. It will be best to keep these inherent pauses or sounds to provide the viewer with the full "flavor" of the individual's character.

33. During the audio mix, make sure music track levels do not overpower dialogue.

Reasons

Music is a very powerful creative device. It can propel a scene forward, slow it down, make the audience feel sad or happy or tense, and so forth. Once you get your program to the point where your music bed is in place, it will be important to regulate the sound levels so the music does not compete with the dialogue or other audio elements in your sequence.

Solutions

Attend to the proper audio level mixing for all audio elements, especially the music. If the music is "source" or **diegetic** (generated within the film world by a radio, live band, .mp3 player, etc.) then be aware that it should play continuously under that scene until the music ends or the scene does. If dialogue is delivered on top of the music bed, then make sure to lower the music level under the spoken words. An audience will accept the fact that the music level drops into the background sounds because they are usually more interested in what the people have to say.

Exceptions

If the location sound is recorded during the documentation of a live event (concert, benefit gala, etc.) then it will be difficult or impossible to lower the captured music levels in the background. Also, if the fictional narrative story calls for the loud music to drown out the spoken word, then keep it hot in the mix for this special purpose.

Working Practices

34. Use a character's cleanly recorded dialogue under his off-screen or over-the-shoulder line delivery.

Reasons

During production, the **sound recordist** may not have the **boom operator** favor the off-screen or over-the-shoulder "shoulder" talent, which means that this "hidden" actor's dialogue will sound weak on the recording while the favored talent's line delivery, given closer to the microphone, will sound stronger.

Solutions

Traditional Master Scene shooting technique should provide multiple shots of the same dialogue delivery as covered from different camera angles. Any wide or two-shot should provide strong audio levels from both characters. Single shots (MS, MCU, CU, etc.) of each character should also yield strong audio recordings of line delivery. Whenever a character is either not on screen or has the back of his head visible in an OTS – but needs to "say" lines – the editor should cut in clean, clear audio track lifted from some other source if the production track is not good for that "off-screen" character. The bad sounding audio for the "off-screen" character is cut out and replaced with good versions of the same script lines. This way, the person the audience is watching gets clean dialogue and the "off-screen" character also gets clean dialogue, albeit from different takes and different audio sources of that performer.

Exceptions

There really should be no exceptions to this guideline. You should always strive to start with the cleanest, clearest, strongest audio signal when you are editing the sound elements for a program. If the sound needs to be modified (made worse) for a special effect within the story, then you should still start with clean sound and degrade it yourself in a controlled fashion.

35. Be aware of proper "on-screen" durations for inter-title and "lower third" graphics.

Reasons

Just as a recorded shot of a person can stay on screen for too long, so can a title or other graphic element. The audience absorbs visual information from the shots as a product of composition, lighting, character facial expressions, colors, etc., but they absorb information from **inter-titles** and identifying **lower thirds** by reading it. If a title is not on screen long enough, it cannot be read and understood. If a title is left on screen for too long, the audience may become vexed waiting for the next shot or the next bit of information.

Solutions

An inter-title that says, "Later that same day..." (only four words) may be on screen for as little as two seconds. An inter-title that consists of several short phrases may require 5, 10, or more seconds, depending on how many words and how complex the visual presentation may be. A general guideline for the editor is to leave a title on the screen for as long as it takes to read through the words three times in a row. This is dependent upon length of written word, of course, and may have to be averaged down or up depending on the importance of the title and the overall timing of the edited program. Inter-titles, traditionally white lettering over a solid black background, are often preceded by a fade to black and followed by a fade from black.

Lower thirds are superimposed identification titles, usually showing a person's name, occupation, or location in news or documentary programming. They appear at the bottom lower third of the screen just a bit after the closer shot of the person speaking is edited into the sequence. The title should stay on screen long enough for the information to be read and digested by the average person, and then it should go away. Often lower third identifying titles like this dissolve on to the screen, stay solid, and then dissolve off – a bit less harsh than a straight cut on and off. It is also customary to use the lower third identifying title on the first appearance of a person in a program. There often is little need to show the title again if the same person is shown again later in your sequence, although this may happen if you wish.

Generally speaking, a title may live on screen at full opacity for as long as needed. The actual duration will be determined by watching the end of the preceding clip, seeing how the title comes on the screen and for how long before it cuts out to the next shot.

Scrubbing the title will not give you the appropriate sense of time. It would be advisable for you to get feedback from several other people who know the project so you can gauge how they feel about the timing of the title elements and lower thirds. Often one-half of a second longer or shorter will make a big difference in helping it feel "right."

Exceptions

There are no real exceptions to this general practice. As the editor of these created graphic elements, you have total control over how long you wish to leave them on screen. After you know the information has been conveyed, it becomes a question of "beats" to determine the appropriate duration.

FIGURE 6.25 Titles and lower third graphics require appropriate timing for each edited piece. Too short and the audience may miss out on information — too long and they may get impatient waiting for the next visual element to appear.

36. If appropriate for your story, make a cut at a loud sound on the audio track.

Reasons

Loud sounds are known to cause many people to blink their eyes. It's like a crash cut.

Solutions

If used wisely and with discretion, an editor may be able to find a point in a scene's development where a loud sound will occur on the audio track. If the picture edit is made at this point, it is likely that the cut transition will be hidden during the blinking process of the audience members who are reacting to the loud sound. This is a bit of a cheat and a bit of a gamble, but it may be effective at the right moment.

Exceptions

One should not cut just any time there is a loud sound on the audio tracks. This is a poor way to construct a good story flow. However, a music video could benefit from this editing pattern if a cut were to be made on the strong drumbeats, for example.

37. Take advantage of the transition point that natural wipes offer when they occur in the footage.

Reasons

Natural wipes occur any time an object moves past the camera lens and momentarily blocks the composition of the frame before it clears out of the way. The movement provides the perfect motivation to make a cut or a wipe to a new shot in the same scene, or to start a new scene.

Solutions

Really thoughtful filmmakers will actually pre-plan the talent blocking of main characters, or more often "extras," to create the natural wipe moment for the editor to use. Other times, a simple happenstance like a van driving through the shot on a long lens exterior set-up can provide the motivation and the physical "image blocker" for the editor to create the natural wipe on his or her own initiative. Regardless of who constructs it, the *natural* wipe is "natural" because it occurs during the shot while it is recorded – the wiping of the image on screen is inherent to the footage. Sometimes, during a complex dolly shot, the camera may crab past columns or pillars in a hotel lobby or a parking garage structure. Even though the objects are solid and unmoving, the camera's movement past them will create a natural wipe on the recorded images. These may become convenient or clever transition points for the editor to use.

Exceptions

Just because the natural wipe occurs within the footage, it does not mean that you must avail yourself of it and cut or wipe at that point, especially if it does not add to the overall scene or story flow.

FIGURE 6.26 An editor can take advantage of the natural wipe within the footage and either cut or wipe to a new shot at that time.

38. Take advantage of the transition point that whip pans offer when they occur in the footage.

Reasons

Much like the natural wipe, the **whip pan** (or **flash pan**) offers a very convenient and visually interesting motivation to transition from one shot to another. If planned by the filmmaker ahead of time, the fast motion blur generated at the end of a shot as the camera quickly spins horizontally will match with a corresponding motion blur at the start of another shot which is supposed to follow. The editor will join the tail blur of shot A to the head blur of shot B and the illusion, when watching the transition play itself through, will be that the motion of the blurring whip hurtles the viewer into a new location or a new scene.

Solutions

These whip pan shots (and much less frequently whip tilts) are usually designed and shot on purpose by the filmmaker during production. Unless there is a great deal of handheld footage that whips quickly left or right, then there will be little opportunity for an editor to create their own whip pan moments, although editing software may provide a cheat with some transition blur effects.

Exceptions

Not all whip pan transitions will play correctly. The tail of shot A and the head of shot B must be whip panning in the same direction and roughly at the same speed for this transition trick to work.

39. Avoid cutting pans and tilts that reverse direction at the cut point.

Reasons

Screen direction and flow of motion have a continuity of their own. When object movement motivates a leading camera pan or tilt in shot A and then shot B reverses that object's movement, a visual "crash" will occur at the cut point. Screen directions will have suddenly switched and the viewer will feel this reversal as a disorientation of visual flow.

Solutions

You will hope that production maintained screen direction and visual continuity while they were shooting the coverage for the scene. If you do not have a continuous direction in the footage between shot A and shot B, then you can either not use shot B or insert some other shot between the two to distract viewers and re-orient their sense of movement so that when shot B comes on the screen, they are not disturbed by the alteration in the pan or tilt's direction of movement.

Exceptions

As a creative practice, it may be worthwhile, given the appropriate topic in a program, to attempt to marry reversing pan or tilt shots to cause the visual crash for effect. A story with strong conflicting themes, an experimental film, or a music video may exhibit such "crash" cuts.

40. Show your edited motion picture to someone else and get feedback.

Reasons

A project worked on for many hours, days, or sometimes months, can become stale to you over time. The fresh eyes of other individuals may help you see weaknesses that you could no longer objectively notice. Parts that you have grown fond of may not actually be suitable to the overall story.

Solutions

It is advisable, but not necessary, for an editor to show his or her work to other people to get their feedback. Just because you, as an editor, think something really works does not mean that it will play the same way for others. Often, showing your work to other people will bring up points that need to be addressed, edits that do not quite work, or even places that are rather successful. Listening to the critical feedback from other people and creating your own solution to those potential problem areas will be an essential skill that you will need to develop as an editor. You may feel that you have done everything right, but the opinions of others bear a certain weight as well – especially if they are paying you.

Exceptions

Unless you live alone in a cave somewhere, you should always make time to have other people review your edited piece. No one should work in a void.

41. Create a continuous motion action edit by cutting during the physical movement in the two matching clips.

Reasons

An audience expects continuous motion when they watch a scene from a story that was shot in the continuity style of filmmaking. The movements of subjects and objects would be constant and uninterrupted in reality, so they should appear to have the same fluidity in a movie of this style. The various shots, from different angles and with different framing, should be cut together to present this illusion of continuous motion. The "blink" of the actual edit is masked by the matching movements from one shot of the coverage of the action to another shot of the continuation of that same action. The cut goes unnoticed by the audience (see Figure 6.27).

Solutions

Perhaps this can be best demonstrated with an example. The simple scene involves a woman sitting at a patio table. As she enjoys the morning, she lifts a mug of coffee and drinks. Shot A is a medium shot of the woman at the table and she lifts her mug of coffee – CUT TO – Shot B, a close-up shot continuing the coffee mug lift and showing the actual sipping of the beverage.

As the medium clip, Shot A, ends you would cut somewhere along the motion path of the woman's arm rising – not before the arm begins to move and not after it has fully brought the mug up to her mouth. This new tail frame, cut during the motion, will inform you where to begin Shot B.

You may start by trying to match the mug's position in the first frame of Shot B exactly to the frame at the end of Shot A. Always back up towards the beginning of Shot A and watch the edit at normal playback speed (scrubbing across the cut will not give you the true timing of the actions even though the object placement may seem correct on the screen).

If there is a jump of some kind (not smooth movement), then experiment with cutting action early or cutting a little later, and judge for yourself. The Trim Tools in your video editing application will make this editing process easier. Most continuous action will benefit from trimming just a few frames at either the tail or the head, or sometimes a bit from both.

Working Practices

Exceptions

Any project that calls for a special visual style, such as jump cuts, or playing with the space/time continuum of actions and reactions, etc., does not always need to follow this practice.

Additionally, if the performance of an actor's dialogue delivery during this scene is particularly engaging and dynamic, then allowing minor gaps in motion continuity may be fine because the audience will most likely be so attentive to the character's words that the glitch in motion may go unnoticed.

FIGURE 6.27 Cutting into the second shot along the action of subject movement will most often make for a smoother transition across the action edit. Viewers ignore the matching action cut as they absorb the new information in the second shot.

42. Keep your rough cut long; do not be tempted to do a finely tuned edit early in the process.

Reasons

No matter what kind of programming you are editing, this guideline applies. Keep your material longer in the first pass or two after the full construction of the assembly edit. Without knowing overall pacing/timing issues or scene-ordering issues, it will be hard to make final decisions about shot, scene, and sequence length. You will be better able to judge what can come out after the entire assembly has been viewed a few times. If it is already missing from the rough cut, then you may be missing out on a better creative opportunity.

Solutions

From the outset, you should include everything from picture and sound tracks that you feel will help properly show/tell the story. At that early stage of editing you really do not know what will be useful or superfluous, so keep it all in. After a pass or two at the entire piece, you will get a much better feel for what works and what does not, what should stay and what should really go.

Often you have much more material than the final **running time** of the program will allow (30-second commercial, 15-minute educational video, 30-minute situation comedy show, 2-hour feature film). Some things that were initially included in your first versions of the edit will stand out as unnecessary. Other times, you will have to make hard choices that call for removing very good segments just to make the final running time cut-off. Regardless, you should always start with the most material and then pare it down ... that is what editing is all about.

Exceptions

Some news packages have extremely short air time and you will not be able to pad out the first cuts and then tweak. You will most likely have very little time to finesse and you will simply have just enough time to cut something together to get it to air in the right time slot.

43. Use a dissolve between *simile* shots.

Reasons

As you may know, a **simile** is a comparison of two unrelated subjects using the words "like" or "as" (e.g. – she was as tough as nails). Two shots that may not have anything in common within the context of the present scene or story can behave like a simile. The dissolve will unite the two different shots and a new meaning is created in the mind of the audience. A straight cut would not unite the subjects of the two different shots; therefore the audience may not understand the filmmakers "literary" intentions. Although a very old and slightly heavy-handed method of visual storytelling, the dissolved simile shot is still effectively used today, particularly in comedies and animations.

Solutions

Sometimes a filmmaker wishes to make a visual simile with two distinctly different shots. In our example, we compare the retired, old farmer to the sleeping old dog. Although the old dog is part of the narrative, a cut to him may not create the sought-after visual connection. A dissolve to him and back to the old man would unite them and allow the audience to understand the visual simile connection.

Exceptions

This sort of visual simile treatment has its origins in the silent cinema and, if used today, can often feel heavy-handed. Through the use of sound and other, less obvious, visual elements, one might be able to convey a similar connection.

FIGURE 6.28 A dissolve across these two shots will help make a connection between them in the mind of a viewer. The old farmer is like a sleeping dog.

44. Use insert shots to cover gaps in continuity, condense or expand time, or reveal important story information.

Reasons

There will arise a need in every editorial process where continuity of action, direction, or dialogue is not quite right across certain edits. There will also be a need for the editor to condense or expand time to help the pacing of a scene. **Insert** shots and **cut-away** shots will help with this. They divert the audience's attention enough from the previous shot without breaking out of the content of the scene in which they appear. The momentary distraction usually serves as enough of a visual break to reset the attention of the audience on the next cut that continues the action or dialogue after the hidden glitch. If a particular person or object needs to be highlighted as "important" to the audience, it can be shown as an insert.

Solutions

The editor will hope to have footage specifically shot for insert or cut-away use, or he or she will have marked certain shots that contain usable insert moments: close-up of a dog, a clock, a photograph, a reaction shot from another character in the scene, etc. Keeping these insert/cut-away clips available will help the editor mask over the continuity issues or help lengthen a moment or condense a longer action by providing a related and believable distraction to the minds of the audience.

Exceptions

Certain footage, for example from long-winded talking head interviews, that has no B-Roll or other related visual material may not offer any opportunity for insert or cut-away shots. If the project does not have the footage and does not call for use of full-frame graphics or titles, then you may be in an editorial quandary.

FIGURE 6.29   The insert shot of the dog allows time to be condensed so the rider can arrive at the cabin that much sooner.

45. Allow a subject to completely exit frame prior to cutting to that same subject in a new film space and time.

Reasons

When a shot showing a person leaving frame at the left or right edges precedes a shot of that same character, but at a new location and at a later film time, it is best to cut away from the first shot just after the subject leaves the frame entirely. It is customary to cut away once the actor's eyes have cleared the edge of frame, because the face and eyes of the actor are what an audience member will be watching, but showing the whole body clear frame allows for a cut to any new location with no need for matching continuous body placement. Screen direction may be maintained, however.

Solutions

As seen in Figure 6.30, shot A ends with the body no longer visible just prior to the cut. Introducing shot B, the viewer will find an empty frame of a new location, and possibly a new time, to analyze. Then the actor or object will enter the frame. This allows something of interest to the viewer to remain on the screen at all times.

Exceptions

You really may not want to leave more of the exiting subject's body on screen at the end of shot A or at the start of shot B, because with too much body visible in both shots it will appear as a jump cut. If an emotional note was just played out in the scene and the character(s) depart, then you may want to linger on the empty location for a beat or two to allow the audience time to soak in that quiet moment.

FIGURE 6.30   If you wish to jump a subject in place and time at a cut point, allow them to clear frame entirely and have the new or in-coming shot start empty. The empty frame will provide new visual data (place and time) to the viewer before the character strides in from the edge of frame.

46. Make appropriate font choices for your titles.

Reason

Whether you have access to fonts just from your computer's operating system or you have downloaded a larger collection of font libraries, you should choose sans serif fonts for most titling purposes in your video editing software. Serifs are those little extra flourishes extending off the major structures that form each letter in an alphabet. Fonts with serifs, particularly when used within interlaced Standard Definition video projects, do not look very good at lower resolutions or when compressed into media files for on-screen playback. The thinness in the design of some of those serif attributes gets lost (see Figure 6.31).

Solution

Select sans serif fonts. You may even wish to make your chosen font **BOLD** and of a point size appropriate to the purpose of the title. Too small and they may not be legible on screen, especially if viewers will be watching your video on tablets or smart phone screens. Spell-check your words and names also. Crazy colors, drop shadows or strokes may complicate things visually. White may often be the simplest and best choice for on-screen titles.

Exceptions

You are free to use any fonts recognized by your video editing software and its titling tool, but the "look" should fit the show and be technically correct (sans serif most often). If you are sharing projects with editing partners across computer systems you should guarantee that the fonts you have selected for your titles also live on the other editing systems – the font data of your titles originates on your local host computer and does not travel with your project.

FIGURE 6.31   The font in title A has serifs and other thin attributes that may not play well on video screens. The font in title B is sans serifs and may look better when used in titles.

47. Review each edit or series of edits as you make them.

Reason

You will not know how the shot transition works if you do not watch it play back after you perform the edit. Without reviewing the edits in your sequence, with real time playback and not scrubbing, you will not be able to appropriately judge any matching action, dialogue continuity, shot timing, overall scene pacing, or so forth.

Solution

After an edit or a series of edits in the assembly stage, you should move your play-head earlier in the timeline and watch across the shots and the cuts that you have just laid in. Watching every single edit may take up some time during this phase, but you need to gauge your progress frequently. During the rough and fine cut stages, you should review each trim and tweak as it is being worked on to know if you are getting the timing that is needed. After you complete an entire scene, it would be wise to sit back and watch it through from beginning to end – note any moments that seem to require more attention.

Exception

Even projects that have a very fast turn-around time will require the edit and review process.

48. Organize your timeline tracks and maintain consistency across projects.

Reason

You can potentially have many different types of video and audio sources that will need to find a home in your sequence. If you organize your video and audio tracks in the timeline so that they contain particular assets, you always know where to place things. Simplicity and clarity lead to efficiency and speed during the edit session.

Solution

Create an order to the track content. Perhaps V1 and V2 are reserved for production video, V3 is for keyed titles, V4 is for keyed imported graphics. On the audio side you may place sync audio (SOTs) on A1 and A2, Voiceover on A3 and A4, Ambient clips (NATs) on A5 and A6, Music tracks on A7 and A8, and SFX on A9 and A10, and so on.

The order of video tracks does matter for image processing with special effects and keyed titles and so forth, but audio tracks can live wherever you wish. The point is that you should figure out an orderly arrangement for media types that fit your workflow and your style. If you maintain this track organization across sequences and across editing jobs, then you will work more efficiently. Capability and speed are valuable skills for an editor to possess.

Exception

Even the most basic of video sequences will still default to production footage living on V1 and sync audio living on A1 and A2. That is an aspect of track media organization.

49. Learn and use the KEYBOARD shortcuts for your video editing application.

Reason

All video editing applications have some keyboard shortcuts available and the professional level software has many that can even be customized per user. Moving the mouse and clicking buttons and menus in the interface is a good way to first figure out how an application functions, but it is time consuming and not entirely elegant. Learning and using the available keyboard shortcuts that execute commands in the application will save time. Speed and efficiency are highly valued in post-production.

Solution

When you are first starting out, take note of the equivalent keyboard command each time you mouse-open a menu to select a function. Try new keyboard shortcuts every time you work in that particular software. Over time you will remember what lives where and you will use them more and more. Most applications will have a master list of keyboard commands in their HELP menu. Some even come with a "cheat sheet" printout that shows the icon for the command on each programmed key cap.

Exception

Certain functions in each video editing application cannot be mapped to keyboard keystrokes, so they may only be selected by using the mouse cursor to click within the interface. Also, depending on your software, the layout of the interface buttons for simple and frequently used commands may make it easier sometimes to just click the mouse. The "Function" keys on certain small keyboard laptops can be a bit snarky at times as well.

Chapter Six – Review

1. Avoid cutting from incorrectly framed head room to a shot with correct head room (or the other way around).
2. Avoid shots where distracting objects appear too close to the subject's head.
3. Avoid shots where the side edges of the frame cut off people's faces or bodies.
4. Cut matching shots rather than unmatched shots in dialogue coverage scenes.
5. When editing drama dialogue, be aware of how and when you edit out a performer's pauses.
6. A reaction shot seems more natural during a phrase or sentence than at the end of it.
7. Do not be too bound by dialogue when looking for a cut point.
8. In a three-person dialogue, beware of cutting from a two-shot to another two-shot.
9. With a single character, try to avoid cutting to the same camera angle in a close-up.
10. When cutting the "rise" action, cut just prior to the eyes exiting top of frame.
11. When editing in a close-up of an action, select a version of the close-up where the action is slower.
12. Understand the visual differences between a tracking dolly shot and a zoom.
13. Beware of shots that track out without motivation.
14. When editing in a pan or a dolly crab move, use the best version that is smooth, well-timed, and leads the subject's movement.
15. Begin and end each pan, tilt, or dolly shot on a static frame when possible.
16. If the subject is moving within a pan, dolly crab, or truck, do not cut to a static shot of the same subject if it is then stationary.
17. Objects, like people, moving in a certain direction have an action line. Do not cross the line while editing coverage or the direction is reversed.
18. Avoid cutting an action edit from a two-shot to another two-shot of the same people.
19. When cutting a telephone conversation together, the subjects should be looking across screen as if looking at one another in the same space.
20. If a character exits frame left, then, for the screen direction of an action edit, the same character should enter the next shot frame right.

21. Beware of screen placement issues with an "object of interest."

22. Cut to a full shot of the location as soon as possible after a series of character close-up shots.

23. On the first entrance of a new subject, edit in a close shot of it.

24. When editing a new scene with new backgrounds, show an establishing shot at the earliest opportunity.

25. Avoid making an action edit from a long shot of a character to a close-up of the same character.

26. Beware of editing the very dramatic cut to black followed with a cut to full picture.

27. At the start of a program, the sound track can lead the visual track.

28. For the end of a program, use the end of the music.

29. Put aside your edited piece for a while and watch it again with fresh eyes.

30. Use close-ups of characters later in a scene for greatest emotional effect.

31. Cut away from a character as soon as his "look" rests upon his object of interest when it's off-screen.

32. In documentary programming, edit out "ums" and "ahs" in interviewee speech.

33. In the audio track levels, make sure music does not overpower dialogue.

34. Use cleanly recorded dialogue under off-screen or over-the-shoulder line delivery.

35. Be aware of proper durations for inter-title and "lower third" graphics.

36. If appropriate, make a cut at a loud sound on the audio track.

37. Take advantage of the transition point that natural wipes offer when they occur in the footage.

38. Take advantage of the transition point that whip pans offer when they occur in the footage.

39. Avoid cutting pans and tilts that reverse or "crash" direction at the cut point.

40. When possible, show your edited program to someone else and get their feedback.

41. Cut during the subject's movement to "hide" the edit in a continuous motion action edit.

42. Keep your rough cut long. Do not be tempted to do a finely tuned edit early in the process.

43. Use a dissolve between *simile* shots to create the conceptual connection between them.

44. Use insert shots to cover gaps in continuity, to condense or expand time, or to highlight a very important object or subject in the plot line of that scene.

45. Allow a subject to completely exit frame prior to cutting to that same subject entering a new film space and time.

46. Make appropriate font choices for your titles, but sans serif usually work best.

47. Review each edit or series of edits as you make them to better assess their efficacy.

48. Organize your timeline tracks and maintain consistency across projects.

49. Learn and use the Keyboard shortcuts for your video editing application.

Chapter Six – Exercises & Projects

1. Conduct a test of most usable fonts. With your video editing application of choice, type the following sentence into the title tool: The quick brown fox jumps over the lazy dog. Run through a series of fonts, colors, point sizes, borders, and drop/depth shadows. See which ones work best over an opaque background and which ones work best keyed over a video background.

2. Record a quick video interview with a friend, family member, or co-worker. Watch the footage and listen for any particular speech pattern, verbal tic, or padding with extraneous sounds or words. Edit out the time-consuming "ums" "ahhs" or extra "like"s. Does it make their responses sound smoother, tighter and more to the point? How did you choose to cover over the picture jump cuts?

3. Practice editing a piece of music to see if you can cleanly cut it down and seamlessly mix the pieces together. Try it with rock, pop, jazz and classical to see which, if any, are easier to handle.

4. Based on the script found in Appendix C, video two people acting out that scene, then edit that scene together. Try to incorporate as many as possible of the applicable guidelines presented here in Chapter 6. If you need to, refer to the shot types discussed in Chapter 2 before you record the video.

Chapter Six – Quiz Yourself

1. What is a traditional Reaction Shot and when and why might you want to edit it into a scene?

2. Why might an Axial Edit (or Punch-In) cause a Jump Cut with those two shots recorded from the same angle on action? When might this be a good thing to do?

3. What are *Simile* shots and what might be the best way to join them together?

4. Why might you want to allow a subject to completely exit frame before cutting to a new time and location where that same subject then enters?

5. If a car exits frame right in Shot A, then how should it enter the frame of the next shot (if you are following the traditional approach to handling screen direction of action)?

6. What is a *natural wipe* and how might you go about constructing one?

7. What is an *insert shot* and how, when, and where can you use it in your edited sequence?

Chapter Seven
Key Take-Aways for New Editors

- Sound and Vision are Partners
- A New Shot Should Contain New Information
- There Should be a Reason for Every Edit
- Pacing Has a Purpose
- Observe the Action Line
- Select the Appropriate Form of Edit
- The Better the Edit, the Less it is Noticed
- Editing is Manipulation
- Role of the Assistant Editor
- Editing is Creating

The material in this last chapter will brief you on some of the key guidelines for any edit session. Regardless of the editing fashion of the day, these practices have been around for quite some time, and although they have evolved somewhat over time, they have stayed true to their original intentions. We are looking to provide some basic ideas for you, the new editors, so that you may absorb these concepts and also move forward with your editing careers. We want you to think on your own as well, and learn by doing. The common grammar presented here gets everybody on the same page. Your editing craft will evolve over time as you creatively expand your skills.

Sound and Vision are Partners

This seems somewhat obvious, but it is surprising how many new editors allow the sound to "fight" the picture. Sound is a partner in the production and must be edited with the same care and attention to detail as the visual elements. The ear and the eye work in unison, supplementing each other's information, so any conflict between the two could cause confusion.

Information on your audio tracks should extend and expand the visual messages of the story. For example, if a shot shows a car passing an "Airport" road sign then, by adding the appropriate airport sounds (jet engines, etc.), the visual message is underscored and reinforced. You deliver a multi-sensory experience to the audience. There is corroboration between the visual and aural information being presented and it helps the audience accept it as "reality." A large truck roaring down a highway, for instance, demands the sound of a large engine.

Sounds can quickly create more "reality" than vision. The eye tends to take what it sees factually, whereas sounds stimulate the brain's imagination centers. This holds especially true for an audience viewing things they have never directly experienced or that cannot happen in our reality. An object disintegrating as it is hit by an alien ray gun isn't real, but the sound you hear makes you believe it is.

This is why musical scoring and sound design (and the quality of the production recordings of dialogue) can be so important to a motion picture experience. Sounds are connected to emotional responses. We process them "viscerally," – from the foreboding you feel in your chest when a deep bass sub-rumble is heard as the hero walks through the dark cave, to the sadness you experience when a single, mournful violin plays when the little girl is taken away to the orphanage.

Consequently, stimulating the ear to help the eye is one of the key tasks of the editor. At its most basic, you keep the dialogue clear and clean so that an audience can hear what people are saying. There is little more aggravating than watching a movie that has dialogue that seems important to the story but the audio track is so muddled or poorly mixed that you cannot hear what people are saying. Frustrating the audience like this is a sure-fire way to get them to "drop out" of the viewing experience.

In more complex manipulations, the sound track can provide important narrative details, augment the "reality" of the story's events, generate emotional reactions in the viewer, and, if sound is laid in that directly contradicts the visuals, it can serve to comment on themes or make an ironical statement. An editor should always remember that sound and vision are both tools to be used in support of one another to help show and tell the story.

Sound and Vision are Partners

A New Shot Should Contain New Information

The success of a good motion picture project is based on the audience's expectation that there will be a continuous supply of visual information. This supply, if it is correctly delivered, will constantly update and increase the visual information of the events of the program that is received by the viewer.

If you are editing an instructional video for a web site, such as how to bake a cake, then you have a pretty good understanding of the flow of information. The recipe for the cake batter and the process of mixing and baking and icing is the pre-built "script" that you can follow. Each shot can show a new step in the process of baking a cake.

Thirty-second television commercials are very exacting in their construction. Airtime is expensive and thirty seconds is a very short window in which to clearly convey your message. The script and storyboards were followed very closely during production because many people had to give approval on just those few details. The editor, although having some freedom to play creatively, is initially bound to the script and boards. Now information has to be present in each shot because you only have so many shots that you could possibly fit, coherently, into a thirty-second spot.

This "predetermined" flow of information can become rather tricky, even with scripted production footage from narrative films and documentaries and so forth. Time is precious to both the presenter and the viewer of motion pictures. If you fail to deliver new information with each shot, then you are not being very efficient with screen time, you are failing to progress the story, and you may be losing the attention of your audience. Keep in mind that "information" can come from the picture track or sound tracks, it can be directly involved with the characters or "story," or it can take the form of intellectual or emotional manipulations that you exercise on your audience. Even shots that just exist to help control pacing or mood can add to those latter manipulations. No matter what, you are constructing an experience for an audience that can readily "tune out" if you do not keep them engaged.

There Should Be a Reason for Every Edit

This convention is linked with *motivation*, one of the six elements of the cut discussed in Chapter Three.

If the shot is good and complete in itself, with a beginning, a middle, and an end, then it may not serve much purpose to cut a section out and replace it – especially if the overall result is not better or more interesting than the original shot. In short, do your best not to cut apart a shot that stands firmly on its own, intact. Sometimes the best choice for an editor to make is to not cut a shot at all, but simply time its entrance and exit within the sequence.

This does not mean that a three-minute monologue from one person to another should not be edited visually. If one person is listening, then that person is likely to make some form of facial or body reaction to what is being said. These **reaction shots** should be shown to help break up the continual, verbal assault of the one character and to provide new information about the listening party (see Figure 7.1). If, however, the person is talking to himself, and there are no reasons to add flashbacks or insert shots, then this uninterrupted monologue may stand unedited. Cutting up a shot such as this just so the audience should have something else to look at is a poor motivation and may only serve to break the monologue's delivery and disturb the audience. If the shot is boring, the fault may lie in the type of shot or the shot composition, the script, or the actor's performance.

FIGURE 7.1 For long monologues, you may wish to cut in a reaction shot to help keep the viewer interested in the proceedings.

Pacing Has a Purpose

In recent history, a very fast paced editing style has become rather widespread. Some trace this back to the "MTV effect," named after the quick cutting of many of the music videos once found on that cable network. Quickly cut sequences, however, especially of action scenes, had been around for years before that. This tendency towards very fast pacing has developed alarmingly to where a shot lasting more than three seconds is viewed by some producers and directors as "boringly long." Quick cuts can be very effective – the reason may have less to do with information and motivation and more to do with the energy or anxiety they can create in the viewing audience.

Pacing obviously depends on the type of production, picture content, and viewing habits of the expected audience. What is acceptable in an action sequence is not acceptable in a love scene. The reason to make the edit should be worthwhile and visible to all. If you capitalize on the motivation and the reason for the edit, the edit will then seem more "natural" and befitting of the mood of the motion picture.

Finally, in deciding the length of a shot, it is essential to give the eyes enough time to read and absorb the visual information. If you are questioning the "proper" duration for a shot, then you could describe, in your mind, what you are seeing in the shot. When viewing the example in Figure 7.2 you could say to yourself, "There is a woman standing in a polka dotted dress, there is a city skyline behind her, there is a gondola on the water, it appears to be daytime and maybe summer. Cut!" And that is the length of the shot.

FIGURE 7.2 One method of deciding shot length is to talk out the basic description of the shot content. If your eyes and brain require that much or that little time to digest the image, then most viewers will comprehend the visuals at about the same rate.

Observe the Action Line

The **action line** (or axis of action) is a mental guide for both directors and editors when using the Master Scene continuity style of filmmaking. It is the imaginary line that cuts through the area of action along talent's sight lines or follows in the direction of an object's movement. With it one establishes the 180-degree arc around the subject. It dictates from which side of that subject one is able to shoot. Editors must make sure that the shots they use in the final edited version stay on the correct side of the line and therefore maintain the established screen direction for the scene.

Crossing the line results in a visual contradiction for the audience. They are confronted with a different viewpoint of the action as screen direction is reversed and this will change their perception of what is happening. It will, in essence, flop the orientation of left and right within the film space (see Figure 7.3).

For example, if a car is traveling from right to left across the screen in Shot A, then the action line becomes the direction of movement. If another shot is taken from the other side of the line, and that shot is then cut next as Shot B, the car will appear to be going from left to right as if it immediately reversed its screen direction. In the film's reality, of course, the car is actually going the same way all of the time. Cutting these two

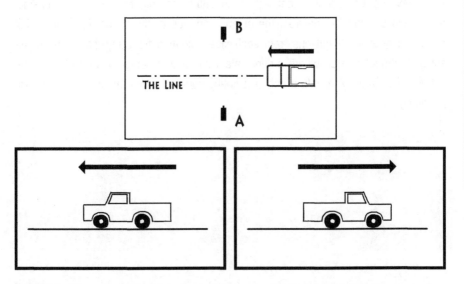

FIGURE 7.3 The camera placement from shot A establishes the axis of action and the subsequent screen direction for the moving vehicle. When the camera is mistakenly moved to the opposite side of the action line, shot B records the vehicle's movement again but this material will appear as a reversal of screen direction when edited together. Edit shots that have respected the 180-degree rule when assembling coverage for a scene.

shots together, the first from one side of the line and the second from the other, will break the visual flow and the viewer may become momentarily confused and ask, "Why is the car now going the opposite way?" (see Figure 7.3).

The editor should only select shots from one side of the line unless the line is seen to change – for example, if the car changes direction on screen during one of the shots, if a POV from inside the car is shown, or if the car exits a shot and then a new, wider re-establishing shot is cut in.

The line also exists for people. A two-shot will establish frame left and frame right, therefore also establishing screen direction, look room, and lines of attention for the two characters. Character A is looking toward frame right and character B is looking toward frame left. Any coverage single shot, such as a medium shot or a medium close-up, should keep the characters on the same sides of the screen and looking in their appropriate directions. The two shots would edit together well (see Figure 7.4).

However, if one of the shots, perhaps the single shot of character B, was shot from the opposite side of the established line, then that person would also appear to be looking toward frame right (see Figure 7.5). Clearly, with both persons looking right, they would appear to be talking to some unseen third person just off-screen. It would not make sense to the audience, who would only be able to account for the two characters. To follow the traditional guidelines of continuity editing, both shots (of characters A and B) should come from the established side of the action line, and within the 180-degree arc – not one from each side. Shooting from anywhere around talent and editing from anywhere around talent can and is being done all of the time, but you should really include it only if it is appropriate for your motion picture's style of editing.

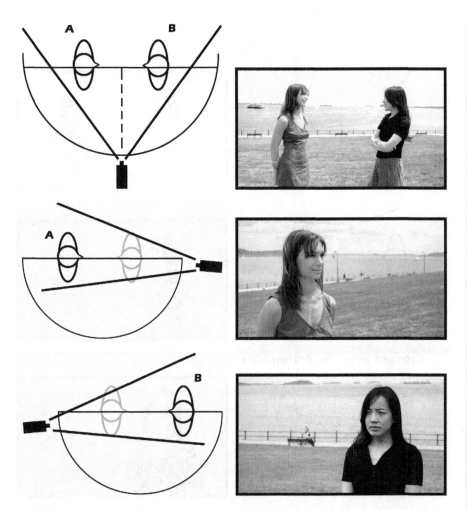

FIGURE 7.4   Shots that respect the action line for people will cut well together. Screen direction is maintained for character A and character B.

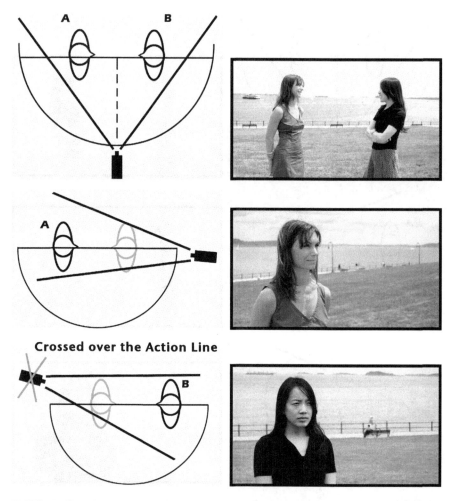

FIGURE 7.5 Shots that do not respect the action line for people will not cut well together. Screen direction is reversed for character B.

Select the Appropriate Form of Edit

If a cut does not create a successful transition between two shots, then it is unlikely that a dissolve or a fade will make it look better. A bad cut is no better than a bad dissolve. Depending on the type of motion media project being edited, it might be possible to use a wipe to make an edit work at an otherwise "sticky" cut point. If a wipe is not appropriate for the show, then you are back to square one. Of course, different genres of visual media call for different treatments at transitions. You will find, at times, that certain edits will just not work.

If two shots will not go together as a cut, then they will certainly not go together as a dissolve. This is because:

- The angle is wrong
- The continuity is wrong
- There is no new information
- There is no motivation
- The shot composition is wrong
- There is a combination of the above

There is very little an editor can do to improve this because most of the time the fault lies within the production footage.

For example, the action line has been mistakenly crossed as in Figure 7.5. Obviously character B is on the wrong side of the frame. As a cut from one shot to the other there will be a blatant jump. It will jar the audience visually. The "technical" interruption of the images' compositions will also then cause a narrative interruption for the viewer and it will not flow smoothly as intended or needed. Clearly, the edit as a cut would be incorrect. If, however, you are condensing time during an event where a straight cut would cause a "jump cut," then an audience would be more accepting of a dissolve on this occasion. For example, one camera angle covers a student taking a difficult exam in a classroom. The shot lasts twelve minutes. You must cut it down, but rather than having jump cuts at the transitions you opt to add dissolves – making the otherwise jumpy edits appear smooth and understandable to the audience.

A similar issue is found in the OTS shots as seen in Figure 7.6. If the editor were to treat this transition between these shots as a dissolve, the edit would be as equally confusing for the viewer. First, because the faces of the man and the woman would superimpose over one another during the dissolve, which would make a viewer wonder whether this visual treatment were somehow symbolic of the couple's union, or perhaps there is some supernatural activity at play, and so forth. Secondly, it would be extremely rare for an editor to use a dissolve during any traditionally edited back-and-forth dialogue scene – there is no reason for it. It just does not make sense.

If an edit should be a cut and it fails as a cut, then the failure might be compounded, even more, as a dissolve (see Figure 7.6).

FIGURE 7.6 The incorrect framing of coverage shots will not work as a straight cut and it is made more complicated by the addition of a dissolve.

The Better the Edit, the Less it is Noticed

This is the ideal situation for most motion media projects. A program that is well edited will result in the edits going unnoticed by the viewer. If the edits are not seen, the story flows more smoothly from beginning to end and keeps the audience engaged.

Sometimes the edits can be very powerful as a result of the images of the edited shots, the category or type of edit, the timing, or the information conveyed. Because they keep the audience engrossed in the experience, they will still not be "seen" and as such will help the visual flow. This is the work of a creative editor.

It is equally true that one bad edit can ruin an entire sequence of shots. The general public (not including filmmakers and those familiar with the technical side of motion picture creation) is not likely to stand up, point at the screen and shout, "Hey! That was a lousy edit." What is more likely to happen is much more subtle and also much more insidious. The average viewer, when experiencing a bad edit, will acknowledge the "glitch"; perhaps not consciously, but that visual or auditory blip will register in their brains or gut as something "not quite right." As they watch the program after the bad edit, their brain may still be trying to justify what it had earlier experienced at the bad cut. The viewer's ability to absorb the new information presented after the bad edit will be compromised.

Remember, it is your job, as the editor, to create a motion media project that will be accepted by an audience. If what you do is not to their liking, or presents picture and sound elements that go beyond the traditional film grammar, they have the right to reject it. If your editing style fits the content of the "story" then they are much more likely to be accepting of it. As many people are very familiar with this "invisible" technique of film editing (cutting that does not purposefully draw attention to itself), you will not go wrong by working in this fashion. Some of the best edits are the ones that no one notices but you, the editor.

Editing is Manipulation

The very nature of the process, constructing a "story" from separate and potentially unrelated sources, is very manipulative. Top that with the goal of providing a particular experience to an audience and it seems like all you are doing is manipulating something or someone. But it's all for a good cause.

A core goal with fictional narrative motion pictures, as opposed to informational and certain fact-based, educational, non-fiction programming, is to engage an audience, get them to care about the lives of others, and have them willingly suspend their disbelief in the actions and events they experience on screen. The content of the shots you edit together, the pacing you provide to those clips, the sounds and music you lay underneath the imagery, all lead to mental, emotional and, often, physical reactions in the viewer. It's part of why people go to the movies and watch television – to be transported somewhere else, to relate to or even care about other "people," and to have their emotions manipulated for a short time in a controlled, safe way. When all of the sources of motion picture creation come together in the right way (story, shots, performance, editing, music, etc.) they will combine to make something very special. Edit for the emotion, and you will win over your audience.

The Role of an Assistant Editor

Like many trades over the centuries, knowledge is passed down from the more experienced editor to the apprentice or assistant editor. One day the assistant knows enough and has proven herself skilled enough to branch out on her own and become a full-blown editor in her own right. Many who start out in the field of video editing get their first job as an assistant editor and work their way up from there.

Responsibilities for assistants can vary widely depending on the type of show produced, the size of the budget, the type of post facility, and so forth. Generally speaking, the assistant is assigned to an editor or an edit suite (the physical room where the editing takes place). He or she may be responsible for acquiring the raw footage, setting up a project in the editing software, capturing the picture and sound files onto the computer and media drives, organizing the bin or folder structure within the project, and helping the editor output any final versions of the edited program for approval copies or eventual mastering of the completed product. The assistant may even get to take a first pass at a pre-edit version of a scene or sequence for the full-time editor to polish – but this is usually done during off hours such as overnights and weekends.

There are numerous nitty-gritty details that go along with any editing facility, such as standardized naming conventions, particular media formats or media drive allocations, and so forth. The assistant editor works with others behind the scenes, as well as in the edit suite, to keep the post-production workflow smooth and easy for the editor. This way the editor can perform the edit free from stress or worry about the organizational and technical elements and focus more energy on the storytelling aspect of the job. Exposure to both sides of the editing process (technical and creative) is a great training ground for the assistant. Observe, ask questions at the appropriate moments, and practice editing. You will be in a good position to transition into the editor's chair when the time comes.

Editing is Creating

As stated earlier in this book, the editor is one of the last people in the creative chain of a motion picture's production. It is his or her job to craft the final version of the program from all the rough picture and sound materials provided by the production team. Furthermore, it is the editor's responsibility to make sure that the types of edits fall within the accepted grammar of the program's genre. If the editing style falls outside the audience's traditional understanding, then the program may not be well received. The audience simply may not get it.

The general terms, topics, and working practices presented in this book offer, to the new editor, the rules and guidelines for basic motion picture editing. Everyone should start out understanding why these guidelines exist and then move forward into the realms of play, experimentation, and innovation with their own editing styles. There are very well-known, experienced directors who, along with their editors, have produced very creditable results in breaking the fundamentals of editing. Some directors use the jump cut to a creative end, others purposefully break the 180-degree rule, and still others choose to provide shots with radical framing or shaky camera or bad color. These are usually creative choices and they are applied to particular sequences for storytelling purposes.

The basic advice and working practices presented in this book are designed to offer new editors some exposure to the many learning points found in the "grammar" of motion picture editing. It will be important for you to understand these conventions, why they were put into practice, and when you might need to use them. But perfect editing grammar is not an end in itself. Breaking the practices to achieve a special result is valid under nearly all circumstances. At least it is worth a try. Certainly, when an editor is seeking to achieve these special circumstances, some general working practices may be changed, ignored, or subverted. Look upon each edit as an opportunity for you to find the most effective and creative way to show your "story." If you don't like the results, the fix is only an "Undo" away.

In Conclusion

No matter what computer software you end up using to perform your digital video edit, remember that you are the editor and the software is just the tool that helps you execute your decisions. As an editor you are, pretty much, the last creative person to touch the visual and auditory components of a project in a major way and, as such, you have an incredible opportunity to help form or re-form the story being told. Whatever you end up cutting, you should strive to combine your picture and sound elements in the best way possible. The shot choices you select, the rhythm and pacing of the individual edits, and the transition choices you make should all serve the story and the characters well and keep the viewing audience engaged, informed, and entertained. In the end, the grammar of the edit is the underlying language used to sew it all together.

Chapter Seven – Review

1. Use sound creatively. It can underscore and enhance the visual data or subvert it in some ironic way. You will provide the audience with a better multi-sensory experience.

2. Keep the viewer interested by providing new visual or aural information in each new shot you edit in a sequence.

3. Find the motivation for each edit. There should be a reason to leave a shot at a certain time and a reason to transition into the beginning of the next shot when you do.

4. Pacing creates energy in the movie. Use the timings of shots to engage and influence your audience.

5. Observe the action line by editing material that holds true to the established screen direction, lines of attention, and lines of motion.

6. Select the appropriate form of edit. Learn when a cut or dissolve or wipe is best and know that sometimes nothing may work to your liking.

7. Good editing often goes unnoticed – this is a compliment, so be proud.

8. Editing is manipulative in its nature. Cut your movies for emotion and performance and you will score every time.

9. An assistant editor performs a variety of important and necessary tasks that help make the entire post-production process possible for the editor. Assisting an established editor is a great way to learn while you work and to become recommended when a new job comes along for you.

10. Learn and understand the basic rules and guidelines of editing grammar and film language, but be prepared to creatively innovate when you know how and why.

Chapter Seven – Exercises & Projects

1. Go edit as many projects as you can, learn a lot, and have fun doing it.

Chapter Seven – Quiz Yourself

1. What is the best job in the whole world? [Answer: Motion Picture Editor]

Appendix A
Helpful Resources for the New Filmmaker

Web Sites

http://www.cinematography.com/

http://www.cinematography.net/

http://www.theasc.com/

http://www.precinemahistory.net/

http://www.joyoffilmediting.com/

http://ace-filmeditors.org/

http://www.artoftheguillotine.com/

http://filmmakeriq.com/

http://www.videomaker.com/

http://www.dofmaster.com/

http://www.filmcontracts.net/

http://www.wga.hu/index1.html

http://www.googleartproject.com/

Books

Cinematography: Theory and Practice
Image Making for Cinematographers and Directors, 2nd Edition
By Blain Brown
(Focal Press, 2011)

Voice & Vision
A Creative Approach to Narrative Film and DV Production, 2nd Edition
By Mick Hurbis-Cherrier
(Focal Press, 2011)

DSLR Cinema
Crafting the Film Look with Video, 2nd Edition
By Kurt Lancaster
(Focal Press, 2012)

The Visual Story
Creating the Visual Structure of Film, TV and Digital Media, 2nd Edition
By Bruce Block
(Focal Press, 2007)

Motion Picture and Video Lighting
2nd Edition
By Blain Brown
(Focal Press, 2007)

Light Science and Magic
An Introduction to Photographic Lighting, 4th Edition
By Fil Hunter, Paul Fuqua, Steven Biver
(Focal Press, 2011)

The Art Direction Handbook for Film
By Michael Rizzo
(Focal Press, 2005)

If It's Purple, Someone's Gonna Die: The Power of Color in Visual Storytelling
By Patti Bellantoni
(Focal Press, 2005)

The Screenwriter's Roadmap
21 Ways to Jumpstart Your Story
By Neil Landau
(Focal Press, 2012)

Directing
Film Techniques and Aesthetics, 5th Edition
By Michael Rabiger, Mick Hurbis-Cherrier
(Focal Press, 2013)

Changing Direction: A Practical Approach to Directing Actors in Film and Theatre
Foreword by Ang Lee
By Lenore DeKoven
(Focal Press, 2006)

Directing the Story
Professional Storytelling and Storyboarding Techniques for Live Action
and Animation
By Francis Glebas
(Focal Press, 2008)

The Technique of Film and Video Editing
History, Theory, and Practice, 5th Edition
By Ken Dancyger
(Focal Press, 2010)

FilmCraft: Editing
By Justin Chang
(Focal Press, 2011)

Make the Cut
A Guide to Becoming a Successful Assistant Editor in Film and TV
By Lori Coleman, Diana Friedberg
(Focal Press, 2010)

Appendix B
Essential Crew Positions for Motion Picture Production

Screenwriter – The person who writes the screenplay, which is either an original idea or an adaptation of an existing property. Not typically involved during the production or post-production phases of the project.

Director – The person in charge of interpreting the story and characters from the screenplay. Generally turns the written words into selected shots. Works with actors to achieve desired characterizations. Collaborates with many other members of the production and post-production teams.

Director of Photography/Cinematographer (DP or DOP) – The person in charge of creating the overall "look" of the film. Chief member of the Camera department. Works with director to select the shots. Creates the lighting scheme for each set-up. Collaborates with Electric, Grip and Art department heads. Often consults on color correction and grading during post-production.

Art Director – The person in charge of the design and construction of the film sets. Collaborates closely with the director, DP, Gaffer and Carpentry team.

Gaffer – The person in charge of the Electrical department. In consultation with the DP, chooses and sets the lighting fixtures that illuminate the film's sets or locations. Responsible for achieving the desired look and levels of light for exposure.

Key Grip – The person in charge of the grips. Works closely with the DP and Gaffer to get the necessary support equipment (for camera and lighting) placed for each shot.

Camera Operator – The person in charge of running the camera. Responsible for ensuring proper framing and double-checking focus during a shot. Sometimes starts and stops the recording process of the camera as well.

Camera Assistant – The person responsible for all camera equipment (bodies, lenses, accessories, batteries, media, etc.). Ensures that everything is clean, cabled, and running correctly. During the take, usually follows focus. Also, often, the keeper of the camera report and logs.

Sound Mixer – The person in charge of running any audio recording equipment on set. Maintains good levels of sound during recording. Coordinates best microphone placement with the set Boom Operator.

Boom Operator – The person in charge of holding or rigging a microphone from a boom pole (telescoping rod that supports the sensitive microphone suspended over the actors as they speak).

Grip – Member of the Grip department. Grips have many responsibilities and are capable of performing many tasks on a film set that involve moving and supporting things.

Dolly Grip – A Grip specifically assigned to build, maintain and move the camera dolly around the film set. May set up and level any tracks or rails needed for the dolly move.

Electric – Member of the Lighting department. Responsible for running the power lines of electricity to all departments on a film set. Hoists, strikes, angles the film lights on set.

Assistant Director – The person on the crew responsible for setting and maintaining the production schedule. The A.D. will verify with all departments that they are ready for a take, call the actors to set for the Director, and call the roll to begin the recording process for a take.

Editor – The person, during post-production, responsible for editing picture and sound elements into the final story that will be experienced by the audience.

Appendix C
Practice Script

The following is a sample script that you may use to practice coverage shooting using the shot types (found in Chapter Two) and all of the editing techniques presented throughout the book. It is referred to as a "contentless scene" – meaning it is purposefully vague and does not follow strict screenplay formatting so that you may interpret freely and maximize your creativity. It may be helpful if you first read the script, make some choices about whom these characters are and what their story is. Those choices will then inform how you may approach shooting and editing the two brief scenes. Have fun.

CHARACTER A

Hey.

CHARACTER B

Hey.

CHARACTER A

How's it going?

CHARACTER B

Good.

CHARACTER A

Cool. Cool. Um, listen – I'm really

sorry about the –

CHARACTER B

Yeah. It's no big deal.

What are you going to do about it, right?

CHARACTER A

Right.

CHARACTER B

Well, I've got to get going.

CHARACTER A

Yeah. Yeah. Me too.

Character B exits — cut to new location. Character B enters followed by Character A.

CHARACTER A

Hey. Hey. Wait up. You forgot this.

CHARACTER B

That's not mine.

[A few hints about this particular script: it should happen in at least two different locations; Character A must be sorry about something that can be represented visually, in some way, in the scene; Character A must try to present Character B with some "forgotten" item, in either a literal sense or in a figurative or symbolic fashion.]

Glossary

30 degree rule—A cousin to the 180 degree rule, this rule suggests that when recording coverage for a scene from differing camera angles within the film set, the camera should be moved around the 180 degree arc at least 30 degrees from one shot to the next to create enough variation on the angle-on-action so that the two different shots will edit together and appear different enough in their framing. A focal length change between set-ups will also help.

4:3—The aspect ratio for standard definition television. Four units wide by three units tall – more square in its visual presentation than the widescreen high definition 16:9 video display.

180 degree line—The imaginary line established by the sight lines of talent within a shot that determines where the 180 degree arc of safe shooting is set up for the camera coverage of that scene. The camera should not be moved to the opposite side of this action line because it will cause a reversal in the established screen direction. See also 180 Degree Rule, Axis of Action, and Sight Line.

180 degree rule—In filmmaking, an imaginary 180 degree arc, or half circle, is established on one side of the shooting set once the camera first records a wide angle on the action in that space. All subsequent shots should be made from within that same semicircle. As screen direction, left and right, for the entire scene is already established, the camera may not photograph the subject from the other side of the circle without causing a reversal in the screen direction.

16:9—The aspect ratio for high definition video. Sixteen units wide by nine units tall – a widescreen display.

50/50—A profile 2-shot, typically in a medium shot or closer, where both subjects look across the screen at one another – especially in dialogue scenes.

Act (noun)—Much like with staged theatre, in long form programming (feature films, episodic television, etc.) the "story" is broken down into several major sections known as acts. In fictional narrative filmmaking, a story will traditionally have three acts loosely termed the set-up, the confrontation, and the resolution.

Action—What the director calls out to signify that the acting for the shot being recorded should begin.

Action line—The imaginary line established by a subject's sight line used to indicate from where on the film set the camera might be placed for recording coverage.

ADR (Automated Dialogue Replacement)—A process where actors record lines of dialogue in a recording studio. Used to replace poor quality or altogether missing production audio. An editor may then use these clean recordings for the actual edit.

Ambience (sound)—The general background sounds of any location where a scene for a film is shot. Examples: school cafeteria, football game arena, subway car, remote forest.

Analog—Not digital in nature. Composed of or designed with a more free-form variant not specifically limited to a single, quantifiable range.

Angle on action—The angle from which a camera views the action on the film set.

Angle of incidence—The angle from which incident light falls upon a film set. A single lighting fixture directly overhead will have a 90 degree (from horizon) angle of incidence.

Angle of view—The field of view encompassed by the light-gathering power of a film camera's lens. A wide angle lens has a wide angle of view. A telephoto lens has a narrower angle of view on the world.

Aperture—In motion picture equipment terms, the aperture refers to the iris or flexible opening of the camera lens that controls how much or how little light is used to expose the image inside the camera. A wide aperture or iris setting lets in a larger amount of light. A smaller aperture lets in less light. On many camera lenses, the aperture can also be fully "stopped down" or closed all the way for total darkness on the image.

Artificial light—Any light generated by a man-made device such as a film light, a desk lamp, or a neon sign.

Aspect ratio—The numerical relationship between the dimensions of width and height for any given visual recording medium. In the example 16:9, the first number, 16, represents the units of measure across the width of a high-definition video frame.

The second number, 9, represents the same units of measure for the height of the same frame.

Assemble edit—The phase during the post-production process where an editor first assembles the raw footage into a basic story structure.

Assistant editor—A support position within a post-production environment. The duties and responsibilities of an AE change with the complexity of the program edited, the budget, and the facility in which the edit is completed. General tasks include capturing and organizing footage within an editing project, attending to the chief editor's needs, authoring proof copies for review and approval, etc.

Atmosphere (sound)—The general background sounds of any location where a scene for a film is shot. Examples: school cafeteria, football game arena, subway car, remote forest.

Atmospherics—Any particulates suspended in the air around a film set or location, such as fog or mist or dust, which will cumulatively obscure the distant background or "catch" and "show" the light in the air.

Attention—The direction in which a subject looks within the film space. Another subject, an inanimate object, or anything that draws his or her gaze may attract the attention of a subject. An imaginary line connects the eyes of the subject and the object of his/her attention and, most often, the audience will trace this line to also see what the subject is observing. See also Sight Lines.

Audio mix—The process of blending together the many different audio tracks used in an edited program such that their levels (volumes) work appropriately together. Spoken dialogue, voice-over narration, music, sound effects, etc., are all blended so they sound good with one another under the picture track.

Axial edit—Cutting two shots together that view the subject from the exact same angle on action but only change the magnification of the subject. See also Cut-In and Punching-In.

Axis of action—The invisible line established by talent sight lines that helps establish what side of the action the camera can record coverage for that scene. The camera should not be moved to the opposite side of this action line because it will cause a reversal in the established screen direction. See 180 Degree Rule, Sight Line, and Imaginary Line.

Background—The zone within a filmed frame that shows the deep space farther away from camera. Most often the background is out of focus, but serves to generate the ambience of the location.

Back light—A light used on a film set placed behind an object but pointed at its backside. It generally serves to help separate the object from the background by providing a rim or halo of light around the edges of the body, head, and hair.

Back timing—Laying in audio from a known and desired end point with a yet-to-be-determined starting point in your program.

Beat—A moment in time. A pause of no precise timing but appropriate for the needs of the edited piece. When strung together, several beats can account for the editor's gut instinct in proper timing of shots, titles, transition effects, and so on.

Binocular vision (human visual system)—Having two eyes located at the front of the head. The slight distance between the two eyes causes the human to see nearby objects from two distinct vantage points. The brain then combines the two distinct images into one picture where the overlapping elements take on a three-dimensional aspect.

Blocking—The planned movement of subjects within the film space and the corresponding movement, if any, of the camera to follow the actions of the moving subjects.

Boom arm—Deriving its name from the armature on a sailing ship's mast, a boom arm is used to swivel and extend the camera's placement to get sweeping shots or keep the camera buoyant without a tripod directly beneath it.

Boom operator (audio recording)—The crew member whose job it is to hold and manipulate the audio recording microphone suspended from a long, telescoping pole usually over the heads of the acting talent.

Break frame—When a recorded object accidentally moves to the edge of the frame and falls outside the visible area of the image.

B-roll—Any visual material acquired for a project (especially news, documentary, and reality) that visually supports the main topic of discussion but does not include important human subjects. Often used to "mask" edits in an interviewee's answers or commentary when used as a cut-away on the picture track.

Business—Any busy work performed by an actor with their hands while acting in a scene.

Butt-cut—A straight edit between two video clips in a sequence with no transition effect such as a dissolve, wipe, or fade.

Camera angle—The angle at which a camera views a particular scene. Camera angles can be based on horizontal camera positioning around the subject or vertical camera positioning below or above the subject.

Camera person/camera operator—The person, man or woman, who physically handles the camera during the shooting. The main responsibility is to maintain proper framing and composition and to verify good focus.

Camera set-up—A place on the film set where a camera is positioned to record a shot. Each time the camera is physically moved to a new position it is considered a new camera set-up. The camera set-up is often associated with a particular shot from the shot list for scene coverage.

Camera support (tripods, etc.)—Any device or piece of film equipment that is used to support the motion picture camera. Tripods, dollies, car mounts, etc., are all examples of various kinds of camera support.

Canted angle—See Dutch Angle.

Charge-coupled device (CCD)—The electronic light sensor built into many video cameras that turns light wave energy into electronic voltages. These voltages get recorded as brightness and color values on a tape, hard drive, or memory card in the camera.

Chiaroscuro—Italian for light/dark. The term is used in the visual arts to talk about the high contrast ratio between light areas of a frame and dark areas. Filmmakers, as well as painters, use this technique to show or hide certain visual elements within their frames.

Clapper board—This is the visual record of the shot which is to be filmed. On the clapper board is marked the scene and the take number, together with other information about the production. The sound of the board "clapped" together is the point at which sound and vision are synchronized together during post-production. If a board is clapped it indicates that sound and vision are being recorded. If the board

Glossary

is held open it indicates that vision only is being recorded. If the board is shown upside down it shows that it was recorded at the end of the shot and is called an "end board" or "tail slate." An end board can be also either clapped or mute. See also Slate.

Clean single—A medium shot to a close-up that contains body parts of only one person even though other characters may be part of the recorded scene around them.

Clip—Any piece of film or segment of digital video media file that will be used in an edited sequence.

Close-up shot—Any detail shot where the object of interest takes up the majority of the frame. Details will be magnified. When photographing a human being, the bottom of frame will just graze the top part of their shoulders and the top edge of frame may just cut off the top part of their head or hair.

CMOS (Complementary metal-oxide semiconductor)—A type of image sensor used in many smaller devices such as cell phones and consumer digital cameras.

Color bars—In video, these are the thick, colored vertical lines that are recorded first on a tape. They are used to calibrate or "line up" the editing machines, so that each time a picture is copied the color is the same. The colors are, from the left of the screen, white, yellow, cyan, green, magenta, red, blue, and black.

Color temperature—Often referenced on the degrees Kelvin scale, color temperature is a measurement of a light's perceived color when compared to the color of light emitted from a "perfect black body" exposed to increasing levels of heat. The color temperature for film lighting is generally accepted as around 3200 degrees Kelvin. Noontime sunlight is generally accepted as around 5600 degrees Kelvin. The lower numbers appear "warm" orange/amber when compared to white and the higher numbers appear "cool" blue.

Complex shot—Any shot that involves talent movement and movement of the camera (pan or tilt).

Composition—In motion picture terms, the artful design employed to place objects of importance within and around the recorded frame.

Continuity—In motion picture production terms: (1) Having actors repeat the same script lines in the same way while performing similar physical actions across multiple takes; (2) making sure that screen direction is followed from one camera set-up to the next; and (3) in post-production, the matching of physical action across a cut point between two shots of coverage for a scene.

Contrast—The range of dark and light tonalities within a film frame.

Contrast ratio—The level of delineation between strong areas of dark and strong areas of light within a film frame as represented in a ratio of two numbers – Key + Fill:Fill.

Coverage—Shooting the same action from multiple angles with different framing at each camera set-up; for example, a dialogue scene between two people may require a wide, establishing shot of the room, a tighter two-shot of both subjects, clean singles of each actor, reciprocal over-the-shoulder shots favoring each actor, cut-aways of hands moving, the clock on the wall, etc.

Crab—When a dolly moves the camera sideways or parallel to the movement/action recorded. The camera lens is most often actually perpendicular to the subjects.

Crane—Much like the large, heavy machinery used in construction, a crane on a film set may raise and move camera or have large lighting units mounted to it from high above the set.

Critical focus—As with the human eye, there can be only one plane or physical slice of reality that is in sharpest focus for the motion picture camera. The plane of critical focus is this slice of space in front of the lens, at a particular distance, that will show any object within that plane to be in true focus. For example, when recording a person's face in a medium close-up their eyes should be in sharpest focus.

Cross cutting—A process in film construction where one plot line of action is intercut with another, potentially related plot line. The audience is given an alternating taste of each action sequence as the "single" scene progresses towards resolution. See also Parallel Editing.

Cross fade—An audio treatment applied to audio edits where the end of one piece of audio is faded down under the rising audio level of the next piece of sound.

Cross the line—Based on the concept inherent to the action line or 180 degree rule, this expression refers to accidentally moving the camera across the line and recording coverage for a scene that will not match established screen direction when edited together. See also Jump the Line.

Cut—(noun) An edit point. (verb) To edit a motion picture.

Cut away (verb)—Editing out of one shot to another shot that is different in subject matter from the previous one, e.g., "cut away from the postman coming through the gate to the dog inside the house, waiting."

Cut-away (noun)—Any shot recorded that allows a break from the main action within a scene. The editor will place a cut-away into an edited scene of shots when a visual break is necessary or when two other shots from the primary coverage will not edit together smoothly.

Cut-in—A tighter shot taken either with a long focal length lens or a closer camera position but along the same lens axis as the original wider shot. See also Axial Edit or Punching-In.

Daylight balance— Emulsion film stock and video cameras may be biased toward seeing the color temperature of daylight as "white" light. When they are set this way, they have a daylight balance of approximately 5500 degrees Kelvin.

Degrees Kelvin—The scale used to indicate a light source's color temperature, ranging roughly from 1000 to 20,000 degrees. Red/orange/amber colored light falls from 1000 to 4000 and bluish light falls from 4500 on up to 20,000.

Depth—The distance from camera receding into the background of the set or location. The illusion of three-dimensional deep space on the two-dimensional film plane.

Depth of field (DOF)—In filmmaking terms, the depth of field refers to a zone, some distance from the camera lens, where any object will appear to be in acceptable focus to the viewing audience. The depth of field lives around the plane of critical focus, appearing one-third in front of and two-thirds behind the point of critical focus instead of being centered equally. Any object outside the depth of field will appear blurry to the viewer. The depth of field may be altered or controlled by changing the distance from the camera to the subject or by adding light to or subtracting light from the subject and changing the lens iris.

Desaturation—In filmmaking, the removal of colors (hues) from an image such that only grayscale values (blacks, grays, whites) are left in the pixels of the image.

Developing shot—Any shot that incorporates elaborate talent movement – a zoom, a pan or tilt, and a camera dolly.

Diegetic—Generated by something within the film world, usually associated with sound elements in a fictional motion picture; for example, a song playing on a juke box in a diner.

Digital Zoom—A camera/lens function which digitally enlarges an image, based on a magnification of the existing pixel data by the camera's processor. The result is often blurry or "pixelated" due to this expansion of limited picture information. A digital blow-up. Differs from an optical zoom, which uses glass lenses to record an actual magnified image of a distant object.

Direct Address—A subjective style of recording motion pictures where the subject looks (and speaks) directly into the camera lens. Used in news reporting, talk shows, game shows, etc.

Director of photography (DP, DOP)—The person on the film's crew who is responsible for the overall look of a motion picture project's recorded image. He or she primarily creates the lighting scheme but may also help in planning the angles, composition, and movement of the camera as well as design details such as color palettes and object textures.

Dirty single—A medium shot to a close-up that contains the main person of interest for the shot that also contains some visible segment of another character who is part of the same scene. The clean single is made "dirty" by having this sliver of another's body part in the frame.

Dissolve—A treatment applied to the visual track of a program at an edit point. While the end of the outgoing shot disappears from the screen, the incoming shot is simultaneously resolving onto the screen.

Dolly—Traditionally, any wheeled device used to move a motion picture camera around a film set either while recording or in between shots. A dolly may be three or four wheeled, travel on the floor, or roll (with special wheels) along straight or curved tracks, or have a telescoping or booming arm that lifts and lowers camera.

Domestic cut-off—The outer 10% of analog transmitted picture information that is cut off at the outside edges of a cathode ray tube television set and not viewable by the in-home audience. Although not as common in the digital age, this phenomenon should be taken into account when composing shots for a project that will be broadcast on television or viewed as a standard definition DVD. Videos encoded for web playback will display full frame.

Dutch angle/Dutch tilt—In filmmaker terms, any shot where the camera is canted or not level with the actual horizon line. The Dutch angle is often used to represent a view of objects or actions that are not quite right, underhanded, diabolical, or disquieting. All horizontal lines within the frame go slightly askew diagonally and, as a result, any true vertical lines will tip in the same direction.

Edit—(noun) The actual cut point between two different clips in a sequence. (verb) To assemble a motion picture from disparate visual and auditory elements.

End frame—Any time the camera has been moving to follow action, the camera should come to a stop before the recorded action ceases. This clean, static frame will be used by the editor to cut away from the moving shot to any other shot that would come next. In a filmed sequence, viewing moving frames cut to static frames can be a very jarring visual cut and this static end frame may help prevent this visual glitch.

Establishing shot—Traditionally the first shot of a new scene in a motion picture. It is a wide shot that reveals the location where the immediately following action will take place. One may quickly learn place, rough time of day, rough time of year, weather conditions, historical era, etc., by seeing this shot.

Exposure—In motion picture camera terms, it is the light needed to create an image on the recording medium (either emulsion film or a video light sensor). If you do not have enough light you will under expose your image and it will appear too dark. If you have too much light you will overexpose your image and it will appear too bright.

Exterior—In film terms, any shot that has to take place outside.

Eye light—A light source placed somewhere in front of talent that reflects off the moist and curved surface of the eye. Sometimes called a "catch" or "life" light, this eye twinkle brings out the sparkle in the eye and often informs an audience that the character is alive and vibrant. Absence of the eye light can mean that a character is no longer living or is hiding something, etc.

Eye-line—The imaginary line that traces across the screen from a talent's eyes to some object of interest. See also Attention or Sight Line.

Eye-line match—When shooting clean single coverage for a two-person dialogue scene, the eyes of the two characters should be looking off frame in the direction of where the other character's head or face would be. Even though both actors may not be sitting next to one another as they were in the wider two-shot, the eye-line of each "looking" at the other must match from shot to shot so there is consistency in the edited scene.

Eye trace—The places on a screen that attract the interest of a viewer's eyes. As the motion picture plays on the screen the audience will move their focus around the composition to find new pieces of information.

Fade—A treatment of an edit point where the screen transitions from a solid color to a full visible image or from a fully visible image into a frame of solid color.

Fade-in (fade up)—Transitioning from a solid black opaque screen to a fully visible image.

Fade-out (fade down)—Transitioning from a fully visible image to a solid black opaque screen.

Fill light—A light of lesser intensity than the key light. It is used to help control contrast on a set but most often on a person's face. It is "filling" in the shadows caused by the dominant key light.

Film gauge—In the world of emulsion film motion pictures, the physical width of the plastic film strip is measured in millimeters (i.e., 16 mm, 35 mm). This measurement of film width is also referred to as the film's gauge.

Film space—The world within the film, both currently presented on screen and "known" to exist within the film's manufactured reality.

Fine cut—A later stage in the editing process where the edited program is very near completion. Any further changes will be minor.

Fisheye lens—A camera lens whose front optical element is so convex (or bulbous, like the eye of a fish) that it can gather light rays from a very wide area around the front of the camera. The resulting image formed while using such a lens often shows a distortion in the exaggerated expansion of physical space, object sizes, and perspective – especially with subjects closer to camera.

Flashback—A device in film construction that jumps the narrative from the present time of the story to an earlier time. Usually used to explain how the current circumstances came about.

Flash pan—A very quick panning action that blurs the image across the film or video frame horizontally. Often used in pairs as a way to transition out of one shot and into the next.

Focal length—The angle of view that a particular lens can record. It is a number, traditionally measured in millimeters (mm), that represents a camera lens' ability to gather and focus light. A lower focal length number (e.g., 10 mm) indicates a wide angle of view. A higher focal length number (e.g., 200 mm) indicates a more narrow field of view where objects further from the camera appear to be magnified and fill more of the frame.

Focus—The state where objects viewed by the camera appear to be sharply edged, well defined, and show clear detail. Anything out of focus is said to be blurry.

Foley—A sound recording practice where "artists" make noises in a studio while they watch the edited motion picture. The sounds they record will replace or augment the sound effects of the film such as footsteps, leather creaks, door knob jiggles, and so on.

Following focus—If a subject moves closer to or further away from the camera but stays within the film frame, often the camera assistant or camera operator must manually control the focus of the recording lens to keep the moving subject in clear, crisp focus. If the subject at the plane of critical focus moves away from that plane and outside the corresponding depth of field, they will get blurry unless the camera assistant follows focus.

Footage—The raw visual material with which the editor works. It is a general name given to the recorded images on the film or video that were created during production, even if the media file counts in Timecode and not feet.

Foreground—The zone within a filmed frame that starts near the camera's lens but ends before it reaches a more distant zone where the main action may be occurring. Any object that exists in the foreground of the recorded frame will obscure everything in the more distant zones out to the infinity point.

Foreshortening—In the visual arts, it is a way that three-dimensional objects are represented on the two-dimensional plane. When pictured from a certain view or perspective, the object may appear compressed and/or distorted from its actual shape; the closer end will appear larger and the farther end will appear smaller.

Fourth wall—In fictional narrative filmmaking, this term means the place from where the camera objectively observes the action on the film set. Because it is possible for the camera to record only three of the four walls within a film set without moving, the fourth wall is the space on set where the camera lives and it is from that privileged place where it observes the action. "Breaking the fourth wall" means that talent has directly addressed the camera lens and therefore the audience.

Frame—The entire rectangular area of the recorded image with zones of top, bottom, left, right, center, and depth.

Front lighting—Any lighting scheme where lights come from above and almost directly behind the camera recording the scene. Talent, when facing toward the camera, will have an overall even lighting that often causes flatness to their features, but may also smooth out surface imperfections.

Geared head—A professional piece of camera support used on dollies, cranes, and tripods that has two spinning geared wheels that allow for very fluid vertical and horizontal movements of the camera. The camera operator must manually crank each gear wheel to maintain the appropriate framing during tilts or pans.

Gel—Heat-resistant sheet of flexible, thin plastic that contains a uniform color. Used to add a "wash" of color on a film set: For example, if the feeling of sunset is required for a shot, an orange/yellow gel can be placed between the lights and the set to give the impression of a warmer sunset color.

Genre – A French term meaning a category within some larger group. In film, the term genre applies to types of movies such as comedy, drama, action, western and so forth.

Golden hour—The moments just after direct sunset but before the ambient light in the sky fades to nighttime darkness. Filmmakers often appreciate the visual quality the soft top light of dusk creates on exterior scenes. Sometimes called the magic hour.

Grip—A film crew member whose job it is to move, place, and tweak any of the various pieces of film equipment used for support of camera, lighting units, or devices used to block light, among other duties. A special dolly grip may be used to rig the dolly tracks and push or pull the dolly/camera during the recording of a shot.

Handheld—Operating the motion picture camera while it is supported in the hands or propped upon the shoulder of the camera operator. The human body acts as the key support device for the camera and is responsible for all movement achieved by the camera during the recording process.

Hard light—A quality of light defined by the presence of strong, parallel rays emitted by the light source. Well-defined, dark shadows are created by hard light.

Head—The common film term for the beginning of a shot, especially during the post-production editing process.

Head room—The free space at the top of the recorded frame above the head of the subject. Any object may have head room. Too much head room will waste valuable space in the frame and not enough may cause your subject to appear cut off or truncated at the top.

High angle shot—Any shot where the camera records the action from a vertical position higher than most objects being recorded; for example, the camera, looking out of a third-floor window of an apartment house, records a car pulling into the driveway down below.

High definition (HD)—A reference to the increased image quality and wider frame size of the more recent digital video format. The increase in vertical line resolution per frame (720 or 1080) increases the sharpness and color intensity of the playback image. All HD formats use square pixels.

High-key lighting—A lighting style where there exists a low contrast ratio between the brightly lit areas and the dark areas of the frame. Overall, even lighting gives proper exposure to most of the set and characters within it. No real dark shadow regions and no real overly bright regions.

HMI—A film lighting fixture whose internal lamp burns in such a way that it emits light that matches daylight/sunlight in color temperature (5500–6000 degrees Kelvin).

Hood mount—A device used to mount a tripod head and camera to the hood of a motor vehicle such that the occupants of the vehicle may be recorded while the vehicle is in motion. Often a large suction cup is employed to help secure the camera rig to the hood.

Horizon line—The distant line that cuts across a film frame horizontally. It is used to help establish the scope of the film space and helps define the top and bottom of the film world.

Imaginary line—The invisible line created by talent sight lines that helps establish what side of the action the camera can record coverage for that scene. The camera should not be moved to the opposite side of this action line because it will cause a reversal in the established screen direction. See also 180 Degree Rule, Sight Line, and Axis of Action.

Incoming picture—At a cut point, there is one shot ending and another beginning. The shot that is beginning after the cut point is the incoming picture.

Insert shot—Any shot inserted into a scene that is not part of the main coverage but relates to the story unfolding.

Interior—In film terms, any shot that has to take place inside.

Inter-titles—A title card or opaque graphic that appears on the screen to convey written information.

Iris—In motion picture equipment terms, the iris refers to the aperture or flexible opening of the camera lens that controls how much or how little light is used to expose the image inside the camera. Some modern video cameras use an electronic iris that controls the amount of light automatically. Most high-end HD and emulsion film lenses use an iris of sliding metal blades that overlap to make the aperture smaller or wider. A marked ring on the lens barrel can manually control the size of the opening.

Jib arm—A piece of motion picture camera support equipment that allows the camera to move around a central fulcrum point, left/right/up/down/diagonal. It may be mounted onto tripod legs or on a dolly.

Jump cut—An anomaly of the edited film when two very similar shots of the same subject are cut together and played. A "jump" in space or time appears to occur that often interrupts the viewer's appreciation of the story.

Jump the line—Based on the concept inherent to the "action line" or 180 degree rule, this expression refers to moving the camera across the line and recording coverage

Glossary

for a scene that will not match established screen direction when edited together. See also Cross the Line.

Key light—The main light source around which the remaining lighting plan is built. Traditionally, on film sets, it is the brightest light that helps illuminate and expose the face of the main talent in the shot.

Kicker light—Any light that hits the talent from a three-quarter backside placement. It often rims just one side of the hair, shoulder, or jaw line.

L-cut—A cut point where the picture track and the sound track(s) are not joined exactly at the same frame. Picture track will last longer and play over the new incoming audio tracks, or a new picture track appears at the cut point and plays over the continuing audio from the outgoing shot. The clip segments around this edit will take on a horizontal "L" shape. See also Split Edit and Lapping.

Lapping (picture and sound)—The practice of editing where corresponding outgoing picture and sound tracks are not cut straight, but are staggered so one is longer and the other is shorter. The same treatment must therefore be given to the incoming picture and sound tracks. See Split Edit and L-Cut.

Legs—An alternate name for a camera tripod.

Lens axis—In motion picture camera terms, it is the central path cutting through the middle of the circular glass found in the camera's lens. Light traveling parallel to the lens axis is collected by the lens and brought into the camera exposing the recording medium. One can trace an imaginary straight line out of the camera's lens (like a laser pointer) and have it fall on the subject being recorded. That subject is now placed along the axis of the lens.

Light meter—A device designed to read and measure the quantity of light falling on a scene or emitted from it. Often used to help set the level of exposure on the film set and, consequently, the setting on the camera's iris.

Line (line of attention)—The imaginary line that connects a subject's gaze to the object of interest viewed by that subject; for example, a man, standing in the entry way of an apartment building, looks at the name plate on the door buzzer. The "line" would be traced from the man's eyes to the name plate on the wall. The next shot may be a close-up of the name plate itself, giving the audience an answer to the question, "What is he looking at?"

Locked-off—The description of a shot where the tripod head pan and tilt controls are locked tight so there will be no movement of the camera. If it was necessary to make adjustments to the frame during shooting, the pan and tilt locks would be loosened slightly for smooth movement.

Log—Generally, all shots are written down while shooting. This list is called a shooting log. During the creation of an editing project, shots that are going to be used from original sources are also logged. After the entire sequence is completed, an edit decision list (an edit log) can also be created to keep track of the shots used and the timecodes associated with their clip segments.

Long shot—When photographing a standing human being, their entire body is visible within the frame and a large amount of the surrounding environment is also visible around them.

Look room/looking room/nose room—When photographing a person it is the space between their face and the farthest edge of the film frame. If a person is positioned frame left and is looking across empty space at frame right, then that empty space is considered the look room or nose room.

Looping (audio recording)—An audio post-production process in which actors re-record better quality dialogue performance in a controlled studio. This new, clean audio track is then edited into the motion picture and appears in sync with the original picture.

Low angle shot—Any shot where the camera records the action from a vertical position lower than most objects recorded; for example, the camera, on a city sidewalk, points up to the tenth floor of an office building to record two men cleaning the windows.

Lower thirds—A title or graphic that appears as a superimposed visual element across the bottom lower third of the screen. Usually used to identify a person or place in a factual news piece or a documentary interview.

Low-key lighting—A lighting style in which a large contrast ratio between the brightly lit areas and the dark areas of the frame exist; for example, film noir used low-key lighting to create deep, dark shadows and single source key lighting for exposure of principal subjects of importance.

Mastering—The process of creating the final version of an edited program that looks and sounds the best and will be used to create other copies for distribution.

Match dissolve—A dissolve between two shots whose visual elements are compositionally similar. Shape, color, mass, or brightness of the outgoing shot will dissolve into visually similar shape, color, mass, or brightness of the incoming shot.

Matching angles/shots (also known as Reciprocating imagery or Answering shots)—When shooting coverage for a scene, each camera set-up favoring each character being covered should be very similar if not identical. One should match the framing, camera height, focal length, lighting, and so forth. When edited together the "matching shots" will balance one another and keep the information presented about each character consistent.

Medium shot—When photographing a standing human being, the bottom of the frame will cut off the person around the waist.

Middle ground—The zone within the depth of a filmed frame where, typically, the majority of the important visual action will take place. Objects in the middle ground may be obscured by other objects in the foreground, but middle ground objects may then also obscure objects far away from camera in the background.

Monocular vision (camera lens)—A visual system in which only one lens takes in and records all data. The three-dimensional aspect of human binocular vision is not present in the monocular vision of the film or video camera.

Montage—(i) The French word for editing. (ii) A series of edits that show an event or events that happen over time but are condensed into a brief episode of screen time. It is usually edited to music. (iii) A sequence of edited film clips that generates a new meaning for the viewer based on the juxtaposition of the individual shots' contents.

MOS—A term applied to shots recorded without sound. It should be noted on the clap slate and on the camera report and camera log. Although originating in the early days of sync sound emulsion film production, it may be used on any project where a camera records the visual images and a separate device records the audio signal. The post-production team knows not to search for a sync sound clip that corresponds to that "MOS" picture clip.

Motivated light—Light, seen on a film set, that appears to be coming from some light source within the created film world.

Natural light—Any light that is made by the sun or fire. Non-man-made sources.

Natural sound (nat sound)—Audio ambience or background sounds recorded on the film set at the time of the picture being recorded.

Natural wipe—Any large visual element that can move across and obscure the frame while recording a shot on a film set or location. This object naturally wipes the frame and blocks the view of the main subject or object of interest.

Negative space—An artistic concept wherein unoccupied or empty space within a composition or arrangement of objects also has mass, weight, and importance and is worth attention.

Neutral density filter—A device that reduces the amount of light entering a camera (density), but does not alter the color temperature of that light (neutral). It is either a glass filter that one can apply to the front of the camera lens or, with many video cameras, a setting within the camera's electronics that replicates the reduced light effect of neutral density glass lens filters.

Noddy—Any reaction shot of a person used as a cut-away. Most often associated with news interviews and some documentary pieces, these shots of heads nodding are usually recorded after the main interview and are edited in to cover up audio edits.

Normal lens—A camera lens whose focal length closely replicates what the field of view and perspective might be on certain objects if those same objects were seen with human eyes.

Objective shooting—A style of filmmaking where the subjects never address the existence of the camera. The camera is a neutral observer not actively participating in the recorded event but simply acting as a viewer of the event for the benefit of the audience.

Outgoing picture—At a cut point, there is one shot ending and another beginning. The shot that is ending prior to the cut point is the outgoing picture.

Overexposed—A state of an image where the bright regions contain no discernable visual data but appear as glowing white zones. The overall tonality of this image may also be lacking in true "black" values, so everything seems gray to white in luminance.

Overheads—Drawings or diagrams of the film set, as seen from above like a bird's-eye-view, that show the placement of camera, lighting equipment, talent, and any set furnishings, etc. These overheads will act as a map for each department to place the necessary equipment in those roughed-out regions of set.

Overlapping action—While shooting coverage for a particular scene, certain actions made by talent will have to be repeated from different camera angles and framings. When cutting the film together, the editor will benefit from having the talent making these repeated movements, or overlapping actions, in multiple shots so when the cut is made it can be made on the movement of the action across the two shots.

Over-the-shoulder (OTS) shot—A shot used in filmmaking where the back of a character's head and one of his/her shoulders create an "L" shape in the left/bottom or right/bottom foreground and act as a "frame" for the full face of another character standing or seated in the middle ground opposite to the first character. This shot is often used when recording a dialogue scene between two people.

Overwrite—Mostly associated with video editing, an edit command that actually writes new frames of picture and/or sound over on top of, and replacing, existing video.

Pan—Short for panoramic. The horizontal movement of the camera, from left to right or right to left, while it is recording action. If using a tripod for camera support, the pan is achieved by loosening the pan lock on the tripod head and using the pan handle to swivel the camera around the central pivot point of the tripod to follow the action or reveal the recorded environment.

Pan and scan—A process used in Standard Definition television broadcasting where an original widescreen motion picture image is cropped down to fit into a 4:3 aspect ratio window (the screen size of SDTV) and slid or panned left and right to help maintain some degree of picture composition. If a widescreen image did not have the pan and scan treatment, it would have to have the letterbox treatment (black bars at top and bottom) to show the entire widescreen aspect ratio inside the squarer 4:3 TV screen.

Pan handle—A tripod head with a horizontal pivot axis allows for the panning action of the camera either left or right. The pan handle is a stick or length of metal tubing that extends off the tripod head and allows the camera operator to control the rate of movement of the camera pan by physically pushing or pulling it around the central axis of the tripod.

Parallel editing—The process of film construction where one plot line of action is inter-cut with another, potentially related plot line such that the audience is given alternating sequences of each simultaneous action throughout a single scene. See also Cross Cutting.

Pedestal—A camera support device that has vertical boom and 360 degree free-wheel capabilities. Most often used on the floor of a television studio.

Picture lock—The phase of editing a motion picture where there will be no more additions to or subtractions from the picture track(s). The duration of the movie will no longer change. From this point forward, the remaining audio track construction and tweaking may take place.

Point of View (POV)—In filmmaking terms, any shot that takes on a subjective vantage. The camera records exactly what one of the characters is seeing. The camera sits in place of the talent, and what it shows to the viewing audience is supposed to represent what the character is actually seeing in the story. It can help an audience relate to that character because they are placed in that character's position; seeing for and as that character.

Point source—A light source that is derived from a specific, localized instance of light generation/emission. A non-diffused light source.

Post-production—The phase of motion picture creation that traditionally happens after all of the action is recorded with a camera (production). Post-production can include picture and sound editing, title and graphics creation, motion effects rendering, color correction, musical scoring, mixing, etc.

Practical—A functional, on-set lighting fixture visible in the recorded shot's frame that may actually help illuminate the set for exposure: For example, a shot of a man sitting down at a desk at night. Upon the desk is a desk lamp whose light illuminates the face of the man.

Pre-production—The period of work on a motion picture project that occurs prior to the start of principal photography (production). Story development, script writing, storyboards, casting, etc. all happen during this phase.

Production—The period of work on a motion picture project that occurs while the scenes are recorded on film or video. This could be as short as a single day for a commercial or music video or last several months for a feature film.

Proscenium style—In theatre as well as motion pictures, a way to stage the action such that it is seen from only one direction. The audience, or in a film's case the camera, views and records the action from only one angle.

Glossary

Pulling focus—Camera lenses that have manual controls for the focus will allow a camera assistant or camera operator to move the plane of critical focus closer to the camera, therefore shifting the distance of the zone that appears to be in sharp focus within the depth of the frame. This is often done to shift focus from one farther object in the frame to one closer object within the frame.

Punching-in—See Axial Edit and Cut-In.

Pushing focus—Camera lenses that have manual controls for the focus will allow a camera assistant or camera operator to move the plane of critical focus further away from the camera, therefore shifting what appears to be in sharp focus within the frame's depth. This is often done to shift focus from a near object in the frame to one further away.

Racking focus—During the recording of a shot that has a shallow depth of field, the camera assistant or camera operator may need to shift focus from one subject in the frame to another. This shifting of planes of focus from one distance away from the camera to another is called racking focus.

Reaction shot—A shot in a scene that comes after some action or line of dialogue. The first shot is the catalyst for the reaction depicted in the second shot. It lets a viewer know how the other characters are reacting to the action, event, or dialogue just shown.

Reformat—Changing the shape, size, and sometimes frame-rate of a motion picture so that it will play on different sized screens or in different countries with alternate standards for motion picture display.

Reveal—Any time the filmmaker shows new, important, or startling visual information on the screen, either through camera movement, talent blocking, or edited shots in post-production. The reveal of information is the payoff after a suspenseful expectation has been established within the story.

Rim light—Any light source whose rays "rim" or "halo" the edges of a subject or an object on the film set, often set somewhere behind the subject.

Room tone—The sound of "silence" that is the underlying tone present in every room or environment where filming takes place. Most sound recordists will capture at least thirty seconds of room tone at every location where filming has occurred. Editors use this tone to fill in gaps of empty space on the audio tracks so it has a continuous level or tone throughout.

Rough cut—An initial stage of program editing that usually comes just after the assemble stage. The story is "roughed" out during this construction phase of the edit.

Rule of thirds—A common guideline of film frame composition where an imaginary grid of lines falls across the frame, both vertically and horizontally, at the mark of thirds. Placing objects along these lines or at the cross points of two of these lines is considered part of the tried and true composition of film images.

Running time—The actual time an entire edited program takes to play through from start to finish.

Safe action line—Related to the analog television domestic cut-off phenomenon, the safe action line is found on many camera viewfinders and is used to keep the important action composed more toward the inner region of the frame. This prevents important action from being cut off.

Scene—A segment of a motion picture that takes place at one location. A scene may comprise many shots from different camera angles or just one shot from one camera set-up.

Screen direction—The direction in which a subject moves across or out of the frame; for example, a person standing at the center of frame suddenly walks out of frame left. The movement to the left is the established screen direction. When the next shot is cut together for the story, the same person should enter the frame from frame right, continuing their journey in the same screen direction – from right to left.

Sequence—A number of shots joined together that depict a particular action or event in a longer program. Sometimes likened to a scene, but a longer scene may have several key sequences play out within it.

Shooting ratio—The amount of material you shoot for a project compared to the amount of material that makes it into the final edit: For example, you shoot fourteen takes of one actor saying a line, but only use one of those takes in the final movie. You have a 14:1 shooting ratio for that one line of dialogue.

Shot—One action or event that is recorded by one camera at one time. A shot is the smallest building block used to edit a motion picture.

Shot list—A list of shots, usually prepared by the director during pre-production, that will act as a guide for what shots are required for best coverage of a scene in a motion picture project. It should show the shot type and may follow a number and letter naming scheme (e.g., Scene 4, Shot C).

Shot-reverse-shot—A term applied to an editing style, where one shot of a particular type (medium close-up) is used on one character, then the same type of shot (medium close-up) is edited next in the sequence to show the other character in the scene. You see the shot, "reverse" the camera angle, and see a matching shot of the other.

Side lighting—A method of applying light to a subject or film set where the lights come from the side, not above or below.

Sight line—The imaginary line that traces the direction in which a subject is looking on screen. Sometimes called a line of attention. Sight line also establishes the line of action and sets up the 180 degree arc for shooting coverage of a scene.

Silhouette—A special way of exposing a shot where the brighter background is correct in its exposure on film but the subject (in the middle ground or foreground) is underexposed and appears as a black shape with no detail but the hard edge "cutout."

Simple shot—Any shot that only contains minor talent movement but uses no zoom, no tilt/pan, no camera dolly, and no booming actions. Locked-off framing.

Slate—(noun) The clapboard used to identify the shot recorded. Often the name of the production, director, DP, the shooting scene, and the date are written on the slate. (verb) Using the clapboard sticks to make a "clapping" sound that will serve as a synchronization point of picture and sound tracks during the edit process.

Slop edit—An assembly edit done very early on in the edit process where speed of creation overrides the precision of the actual cut points. The general structure of the story is hastily assembled.

Slow motion—Any treatment in film or video where the actual time of an event to occur is slowed down considerably so it lasts longer in screen time and more detail of the action can be analyzed by the viewer.

Smash cut—An abrupt and often jarring transition between two contrasting actions or moods that happen at different times and/or places.

Soft light—Any light that has diffused, non-parallel rays. Strong shadows are very rare if one uses soft light to illuminate talent.

Sound bridge—An audio treatment given to a cut point where either the sound of the outgoing shot continues underneath the new image of the incoming picture track or the new audio of the incoming shot begins to play before the picture of the outgoing shot leaves the screen.

Sound design—The process of building audio tracks that act to augment and enhance the physical actions seen on the screen and the sounds from the environments in which the story's action takes place. These sounds may be actual sounds or fabricated to generate a hyper-reality of the audio elements in a program.

Sound on tape (SOT)—Most often associated with the spoken word from news reporters or documentary interviewees. SOTs are the sound bites.

Sound recordist—The person on a film crew responsible for recording spoken dialogue, ambience, and room tone.

Splice—(verb) To cut two shots together. (noun) Originated when physical strips of film were taped or glued together to join them at an edit point. The actual cut point on a strip of film where two pieces are glued or taped together.

Splicer—In film, the footage is physically cut with a small machine called a splicer and the pictures are "spliced" together with glue or special transparent tape.

Split edit—A cut point where the picture track and the sound track(s) are not joined exactly at the same frame. Picture track will last longer and play over the new incoming audio tracks, or a new picture track appears at the cut point and plays over the continuing audio from the outgoing shot. The clip segments around this edit will take on a horizontal "L" shape. See also L-Cut and Lapping.

Spot—Slang for a television commercial advertisement.

Spreader (tripod)—The three legs of a tripod are often attached to a rubber or metal device to keep the legs from splaying too far apart while the heavy camera sits atop the tripod head. This three-branched brace allows for greater stability, especially as the tripod legs are spread further and further apart to get the camera lower to the ground.

Staging—The placement of talent and objects within the film set.

Standard definition (SD)—A reference to the normal image quality and frame size of most televisions around the world during the twentieth century. Limitations in broadcast bandwidth, among other technological reasons, required a low resolution image (525-line NTSC or 576-line PAL) of the 4:3 aspect ratio for television reception in the home.

Start frame—Whenever the camera needs to move in order to follow action, the camera should begin recording, stay stationary for a few moments while the action begins, and then start to move to follow the action. The start frame can be useful to the editor of the film so that the shot will have a static frame to start with at the beginning of the cut. Static frames cut to moving frames can be a jarring visual experience and this static start frame may help prevent this from occurring.

Sticks—An alternate name for (i) a camera tripod and (ii) the clapboard or slate used to mark the synchronization point of picture and sound being recorded.

Storyboards—Drawings often done during pre-production of a motion picture that represent the best guess of what the ultimate framing and movement of camera shots will be when the film goes into production. These "comic book" style illustrations will act as a template for the creative team when principal photography begins.

Straight cut—An edit point where the picture track and sound track(s) are cut and joined at the same moment in time. See also Butt-Cut.

Subjective shooting—A style of filmmaking where the talent addresses the camera straight into the lens (as in news broadcasting) or when the camera records exactly what a character is observing in a fictional narrative, as with the point-of-view shot.

Suite—A small room in which editing machines are kept and used. The actual editing of the program will often occur in this private, dark, quiet room so the editor can stay focused on the footage and the sound elements without outside disturbances.

Superimposition—When an image of less than 100% opacity is placed on top of another image. This is like a dissolve that lasts for a longer time on screen.

Sync—Short for synchronous or synchronized. In film work, it refers to how the audio tracks play in corresponding time with the picture track. When you see the mouth move you hear the appropriate audio play at the exact same time.

Tail—The common film term for the end of a shot, especially during the post-production editing process.

Tail slate—Often used while recording documentary footage, a tail slate is the process of identifying the shot and "clapping" the slate after the action has been recorded but before the camera stops rolling. The slate is physically held upside-down to visually indicate a Tail Slate.

Take—Each action, event, or dialogue delivery recorded in a shot may need to be repeated until its technical and creative aspects are done to the satisfaction of the filmmakers. Each time the camera rolls to record this repeated event is called a "take." Takes are traditionally numbered starting at "one."

Taking lens—The active lens on a motion picture or video camera that is actually collecting, focusing, and controlling the light for the recording of the image. On certain models of emulsion film motion picture cameras there can be more than one lens mounted on the camera body. Most video cameras have only one lens and that would be the "taking" lens.

Talking head—Any medium close-up shot or closer that frames one person's head and shoulders. Usually associated with documentaries, news, and interview footage.

Three point lighting—A basic but widely used lighting method where you employ a key light for main exposure on one side of talent, a fill light for contrast control on the opposite side, and a back light for subject/background separation.

Tilt—The vertical movement, either down–up or up–down, of the camera while it is recording action. If using a tripod for camera support, the tilt is achieved by loosening the tilt lock on the tripod head and using the pan handle to swing the camera lens up or down to follow the vertical action or reveal the recorded environment.

Timecode—A counting scheme based on hours, minutes, seconds, and frames that is used to keep track of image and sound placement on video, digital media files, and editing software.

Track in/out—Moving the camera into set or pulling camera out of set, usually atop a dolly on tracks. Also known as trucking in and trucking out.

Tracks/rail—Much like railroad tracks, these small-scale metal rails are used to smoothly roll a dolly across surfaces, either inside or outside, to get a moving shot.

Tripod—A three-legged device, often with telescoping legs, used to support and steady the camera for motion picture shooting. The camera attaches to a device capable of vertical and horizontal axis movement called the tripod head, which sits atop the balancing legs.

Tripod head—The device, usually mounted on top of tripod legs, to which one attaches the camera. The head may have panning and tilting functionality.

Truck in/out—Moving the camera into set or pulling camera out of set, usually atop a dolly on tracks. Also known as tracking in and tracking out.

Tungsten balanced— Film and video cameras may be biased toward seeing the color temperature of tungsten lamps (aka film lights) as "white" light. When they are set this way, they have a tungsten balance at approximately 3200 degrees Kelvin.

Two-shot—Any shot that contains the bodies (or body parts) of two people.

Underexposed—A state of an image where the dark regions contain no discernable visual data but appear as deep black zones. The overall tonality of this image may also be lacking in true "white" values, so everything seems gray down to black in luminance.

Vanishing point—A long-established technique in the visual arts where opposing diagonal lines converge at the horizon line to indicate the inclusion of a great distance in the image's environment. It is an illusion used to help represent three-dimensional space on a two-dimensional surface.

Vari-focal lens—Another name for a "zoom" lens. A lens that has multiple glass elements that allow it to catch light from various focal lengths or angles of view of a scene.

Video format—A video comprises recorded electronic voltage fluctuations or digital bit data that represent picture and sound information. Video cameras are manufactured to record that data onto a tape or memory card in a particular way. The shape, amount of data, frame rate, color information, and so forth that gets recorded are determined by the technologies inside the video camera. Examples include NTSC-525 line, PAL, HD-1080i, HD-720p.

Visible spectrum—The zone in electromagnetic energy waves that appears to our eyes and brains as colored light.

Voice-over narration—An edited program may require the voice of an unseen narrator who provides important information or commentary about the story that is unfolding. The voice is heard "over" the pictures and the Nats.

Voice slate—A practice used at the head of a shot after the camera is rolling and before the director calls "action." Often, a camera assistant will verbally speak the scene and take number to identify the audio data that may be recorded separately from the picture.

Whip pan—An extremely quick panning action that will cause severe motion blur on the recorded image. Often used to exit a scene and then quickly begin another at a different time or place.

Wipe—An editing transition where an incoming shot's image literally wipes the existing outgoing shot's image from the screen.

Workflow—A plan or methodology that maps the organizational flow of picture and sound data from the production through numerous post-production phases and ultimately to a finished product that is distributed for viewing. Managing a clear digital media file workflow is very important to the efficient completion of any project.

Zoom lens—A camera lens whose multiple glass lens element construction and telescoping barrel design allow it to gather light from a wide range or field of view and also from a very narrow (more magnified) field of view. The focal length of the lens is altered by changing the distances of the optical elements contained within the lens barrel itself. Most modern video cameras have built-in optical zoom lenses that can be adjusted from wide to telephoto with the touch of a button.

Index